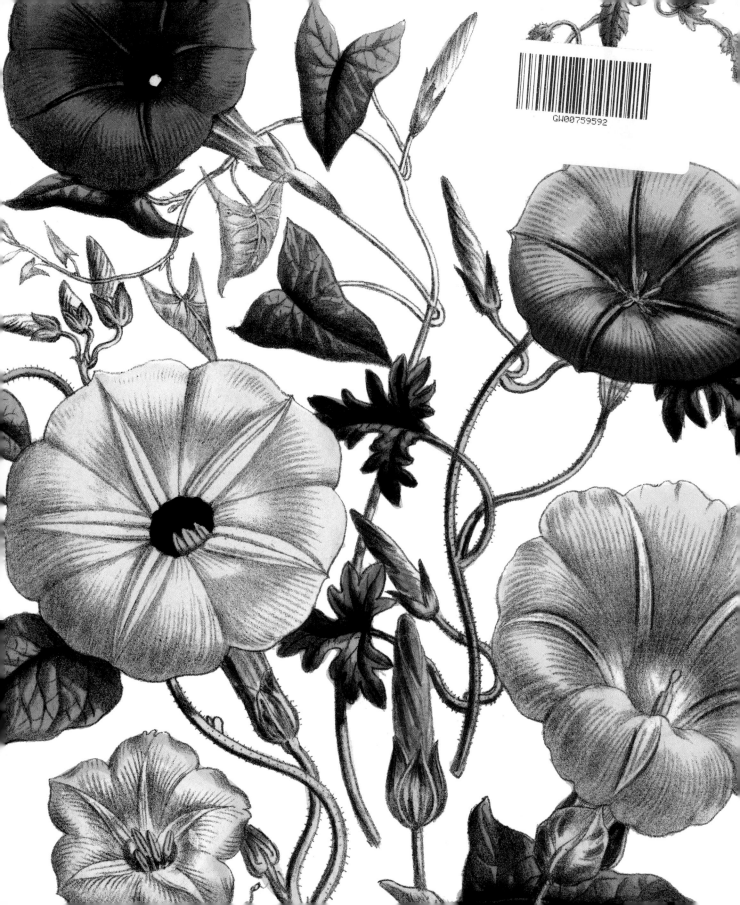

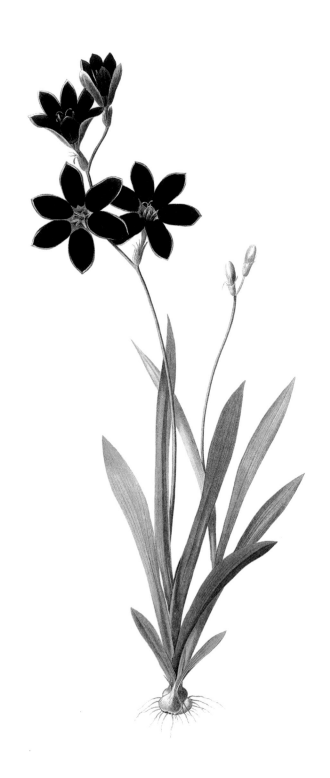

FLOWERS

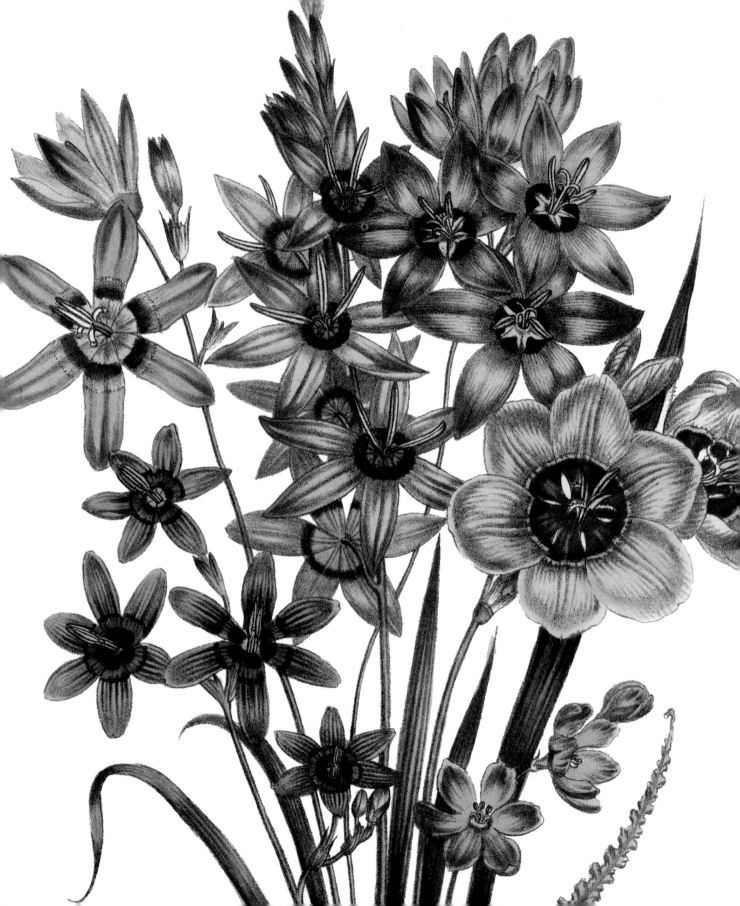

FLOWERS

DOVERPICTURA

DOVER PUBLICATIONS, INC. | Mineola, New York

Selected and designed by Joel Waldrep and Alan Weller.

Flowers is a new work, first published by Dover Publications, Inc.,
in 2007.

The CD-ROM file names correspond to the images in the book. All of the artwork
stored on the CD-ROM can be imported directly into a wide range of design and
word-processing programs on either Windows or Macintosh platforms. No further
installation is necessary.

ISBN 10: 0-486-99887-8
ISBN 13: 978-0-486-99887-9

Manufactured in the United States of America
Dover Publications, Inc., 31 East 2nd Street, Mineola, NY 11501
www.doverpublications.com

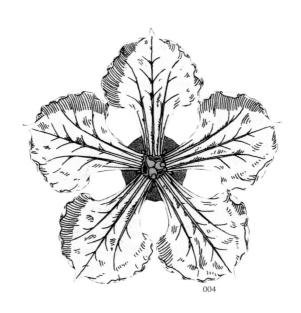

004

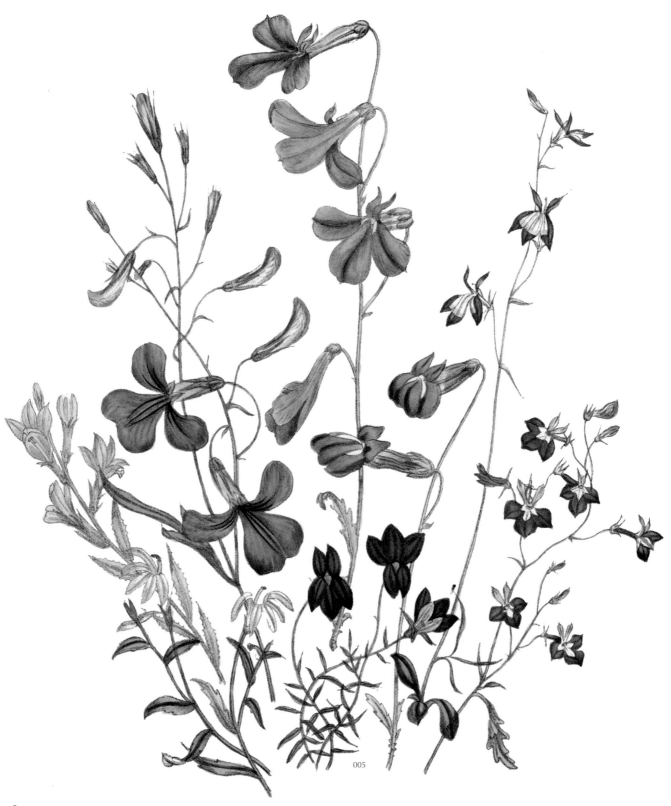

005

8

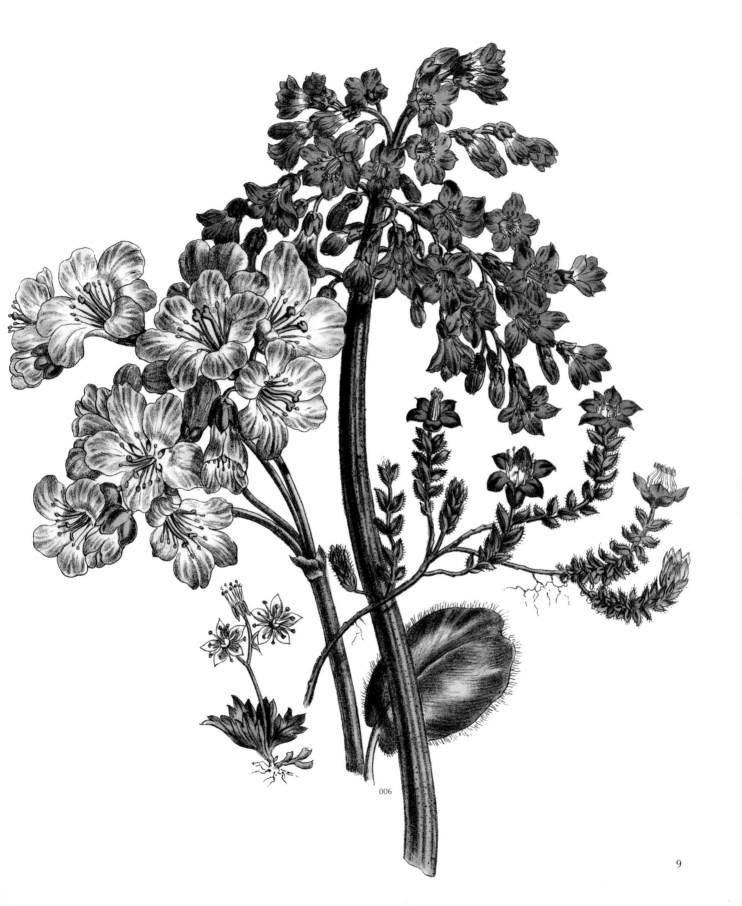

006

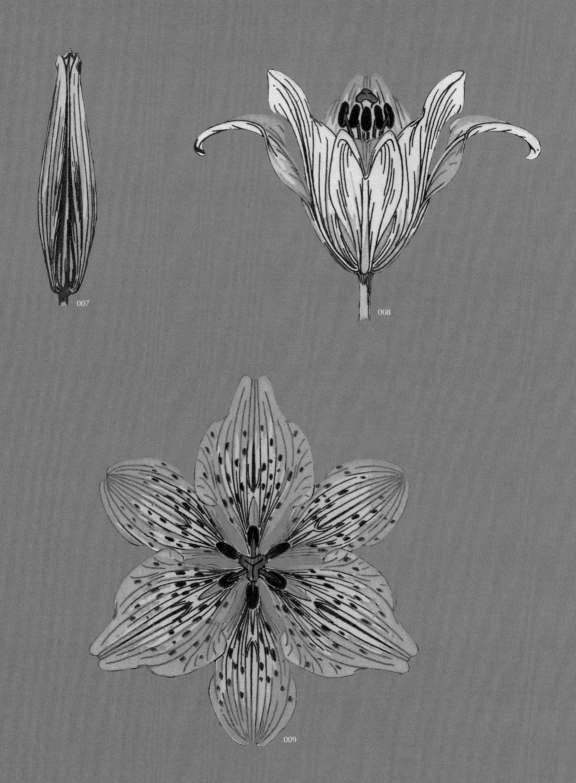

007

008

009

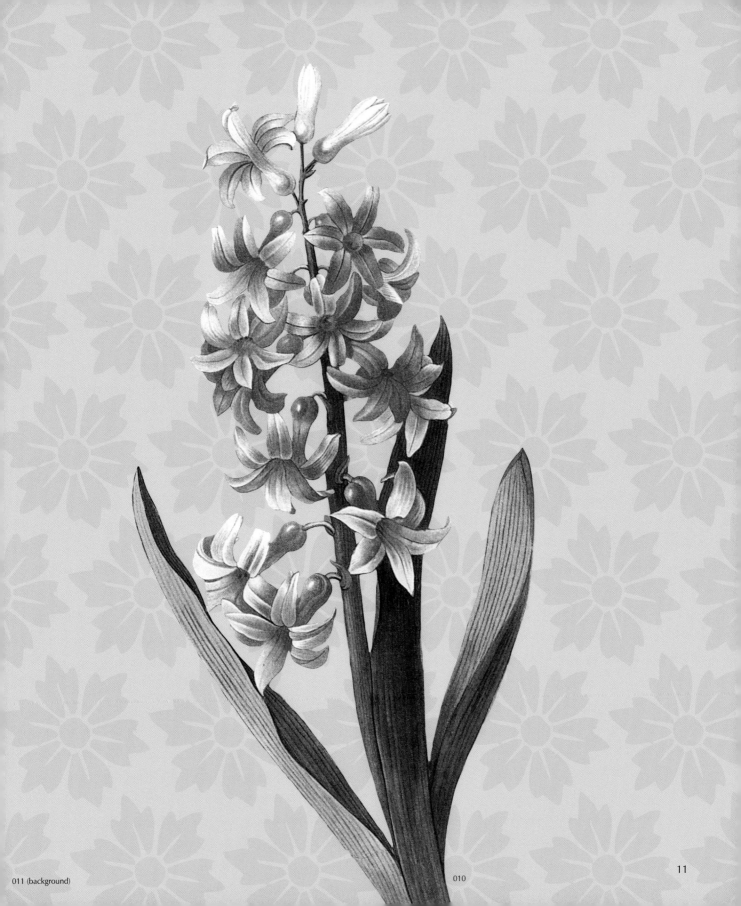

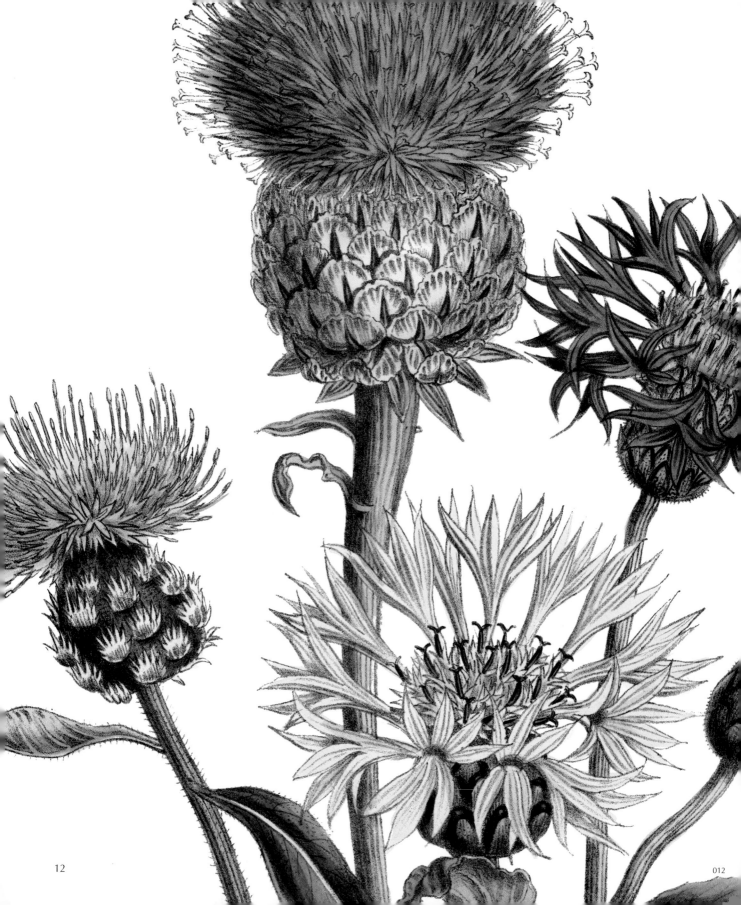

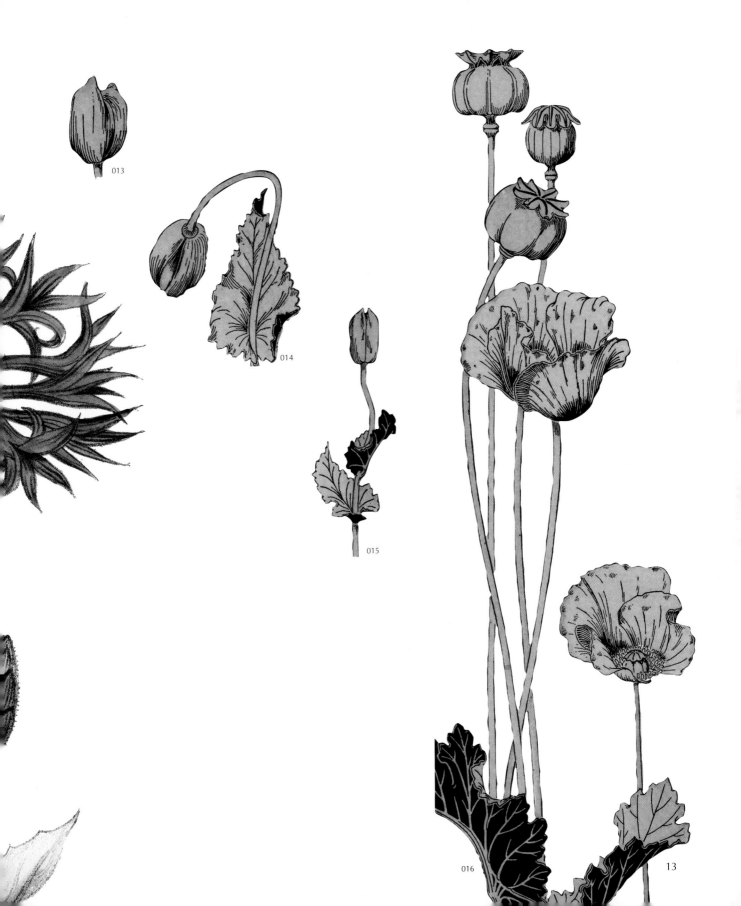

013

014

015

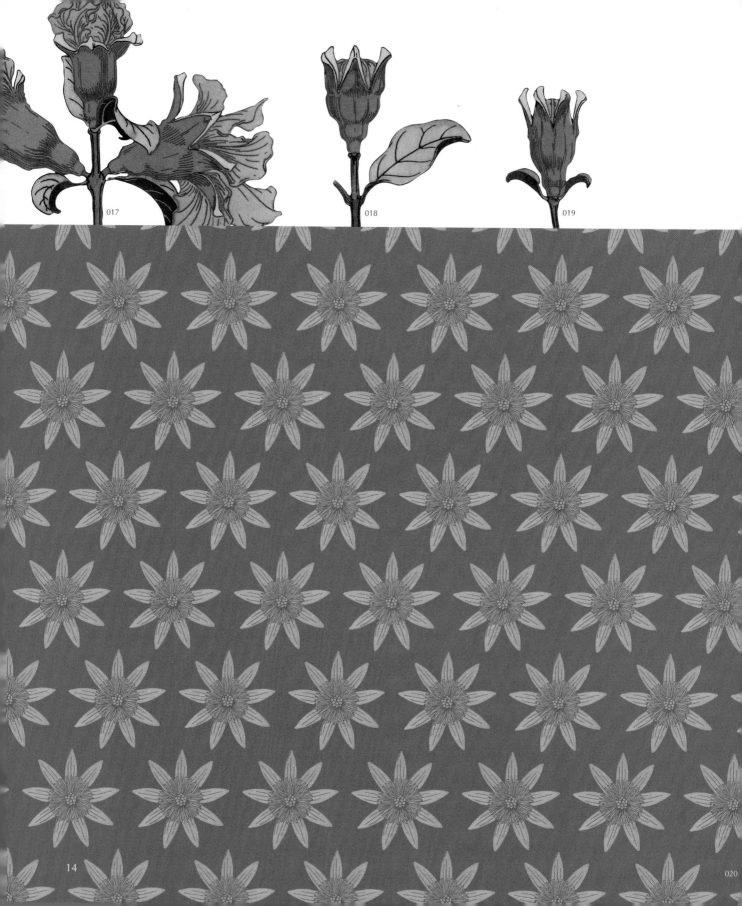

017

018

019

020

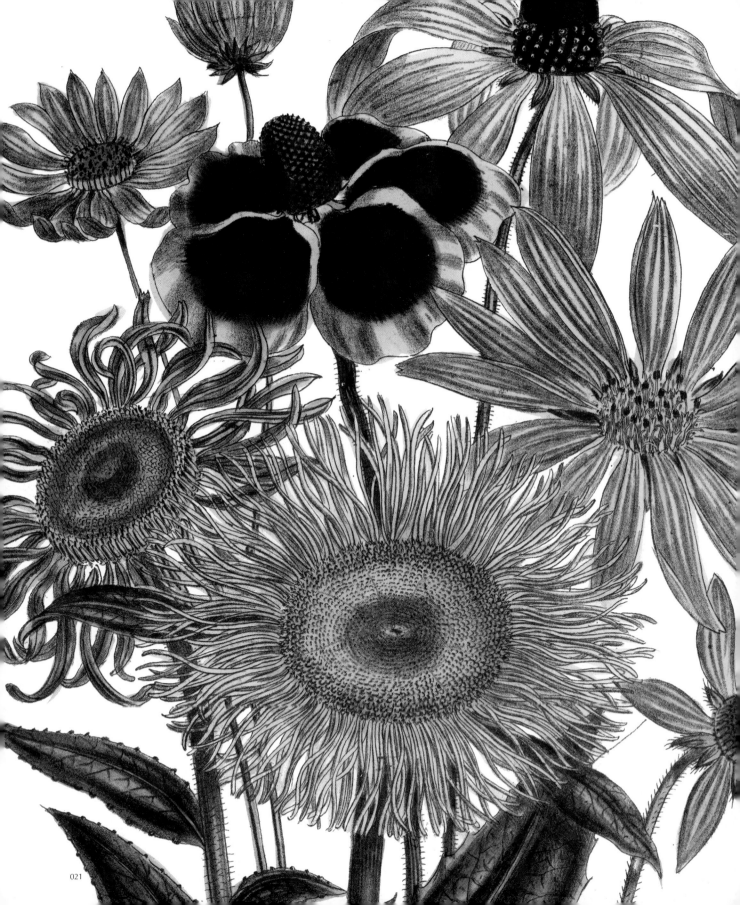

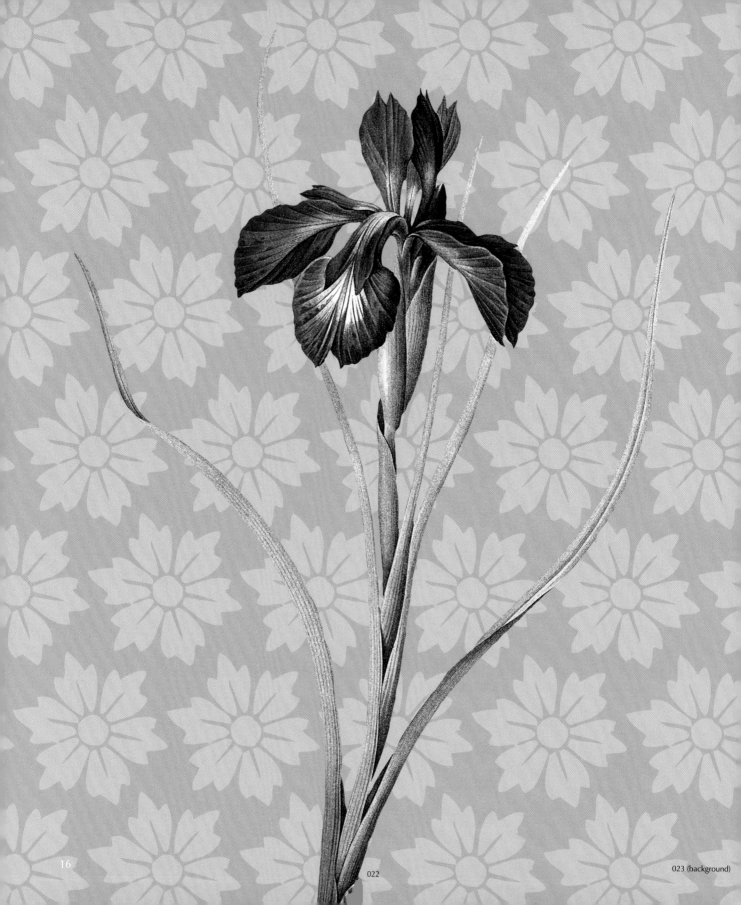

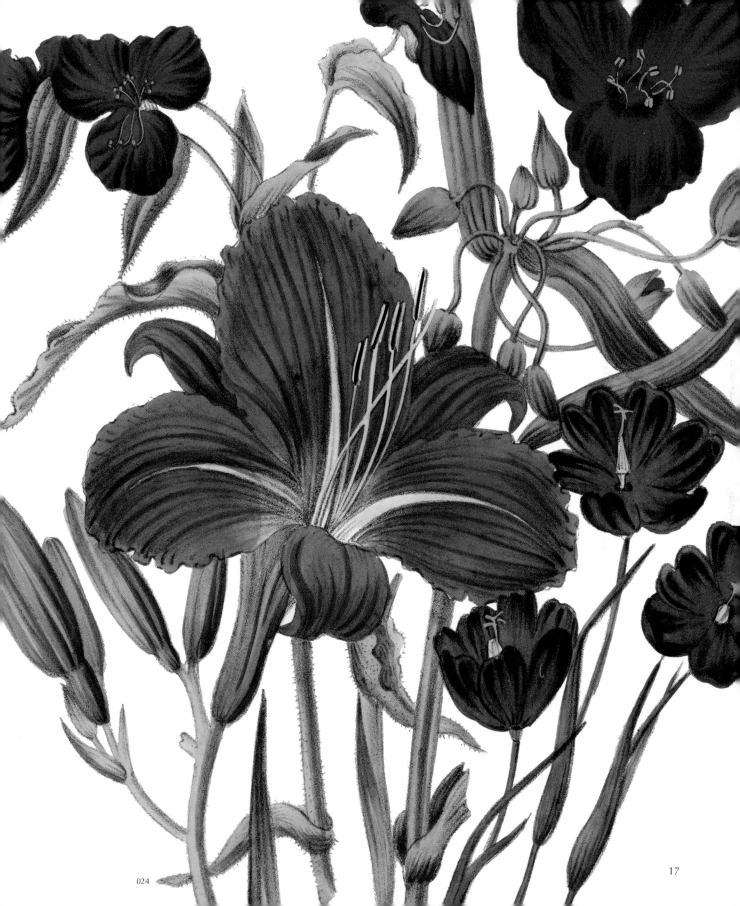

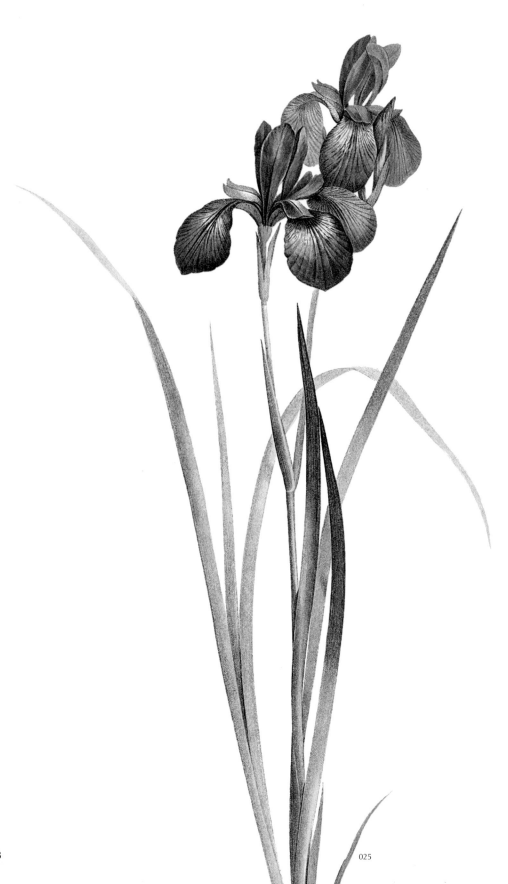

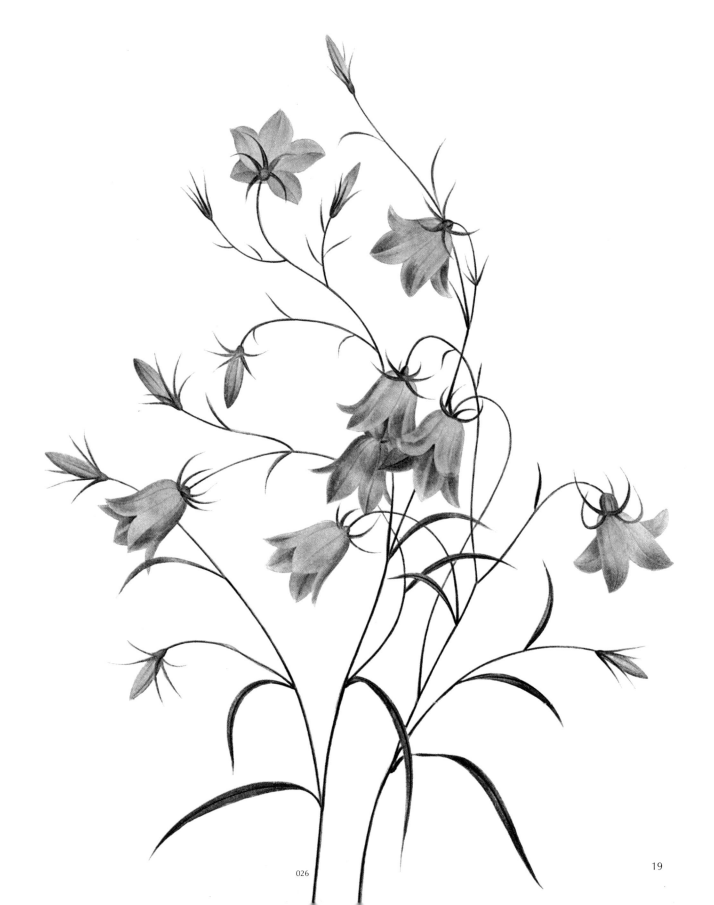

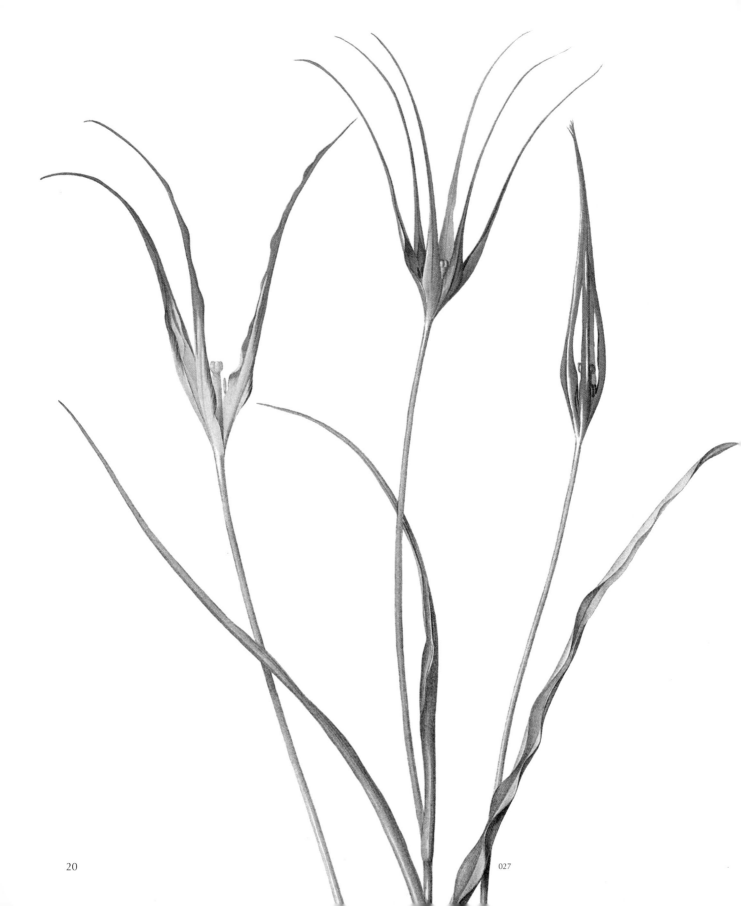

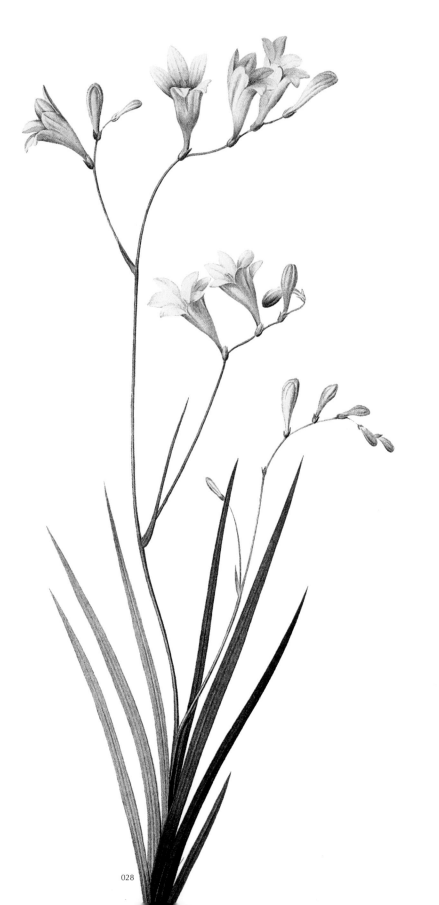

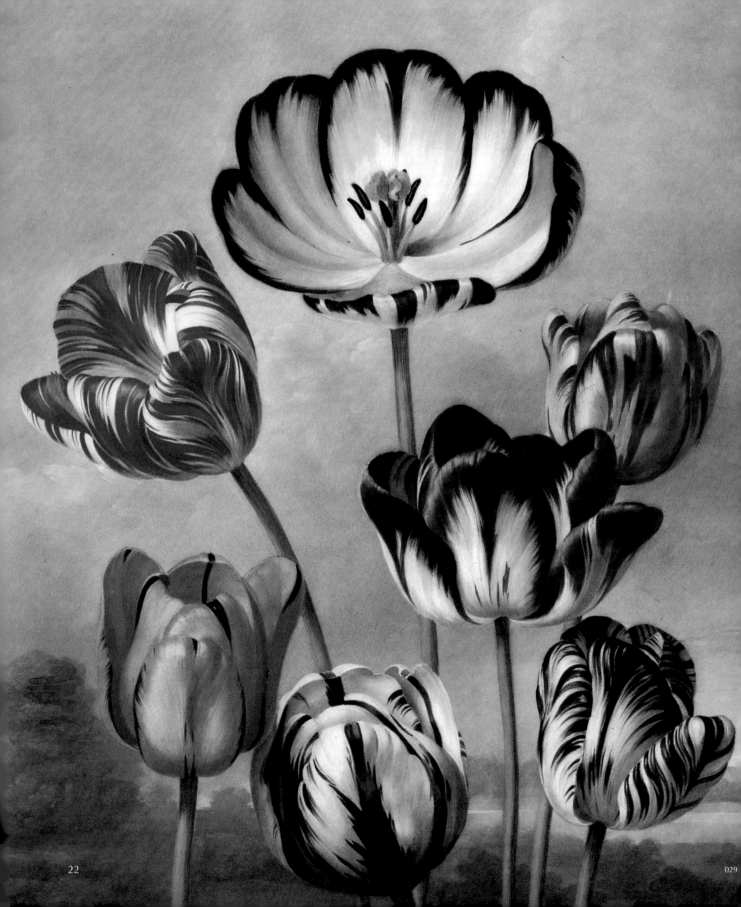

030

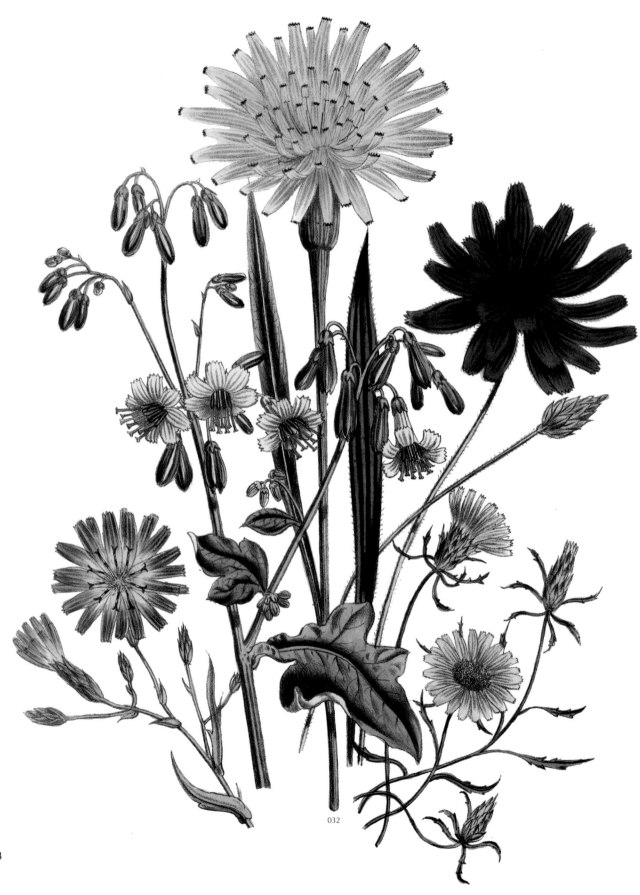

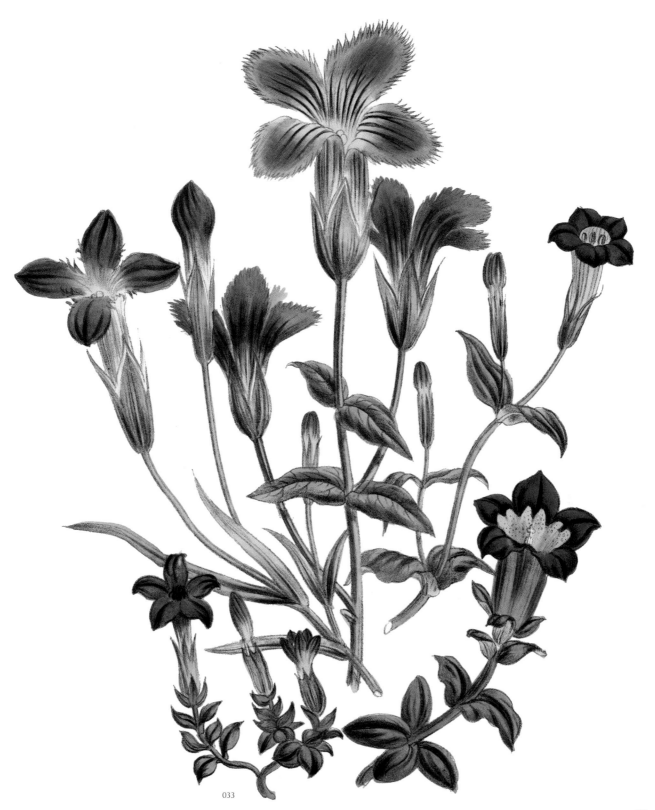

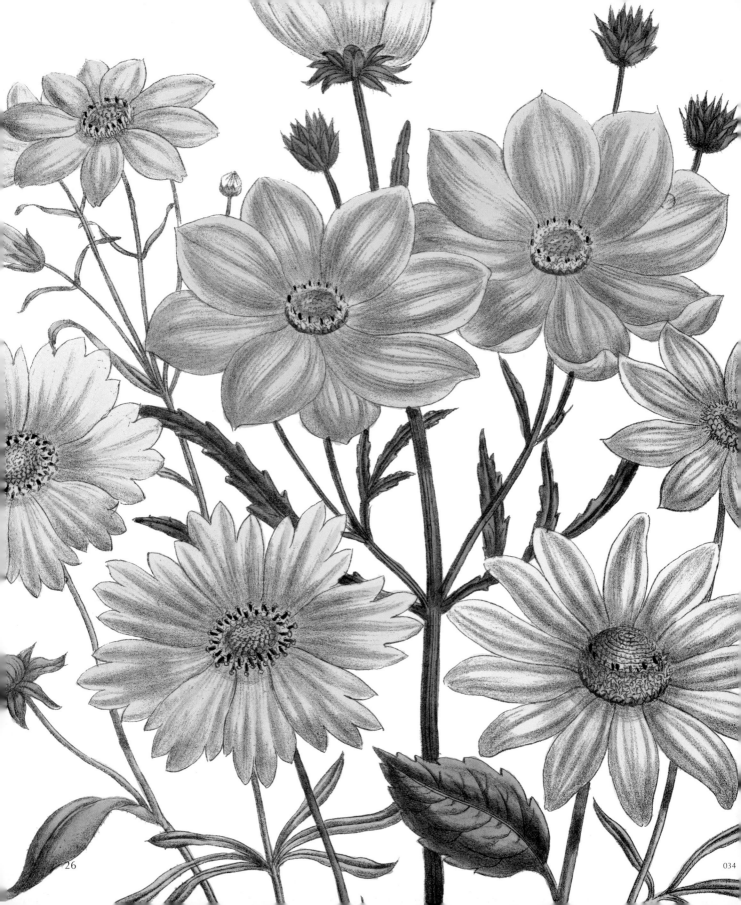

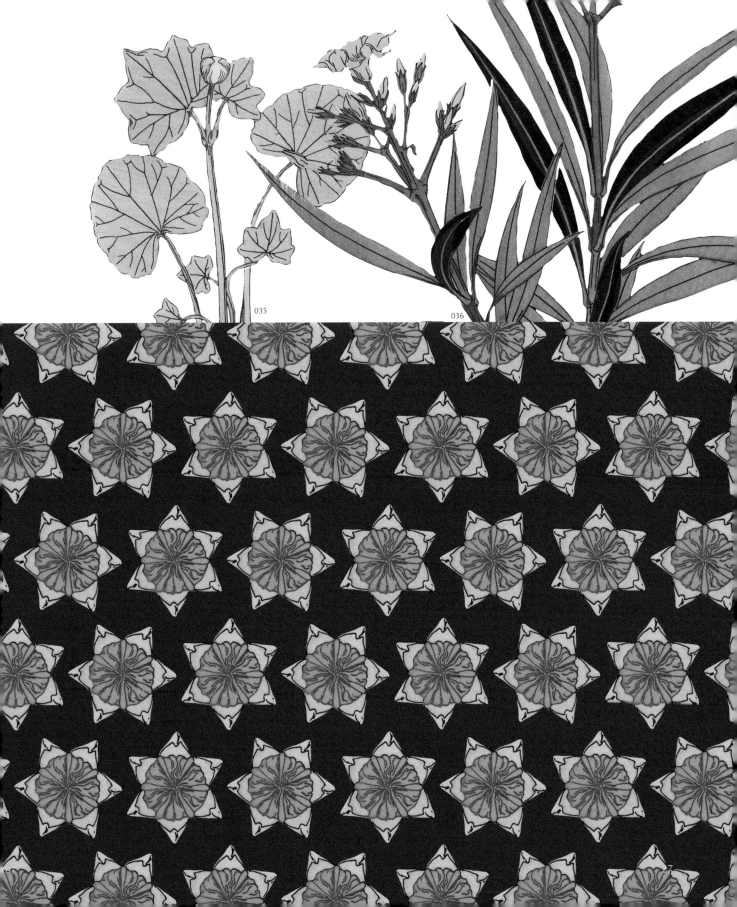

035

036

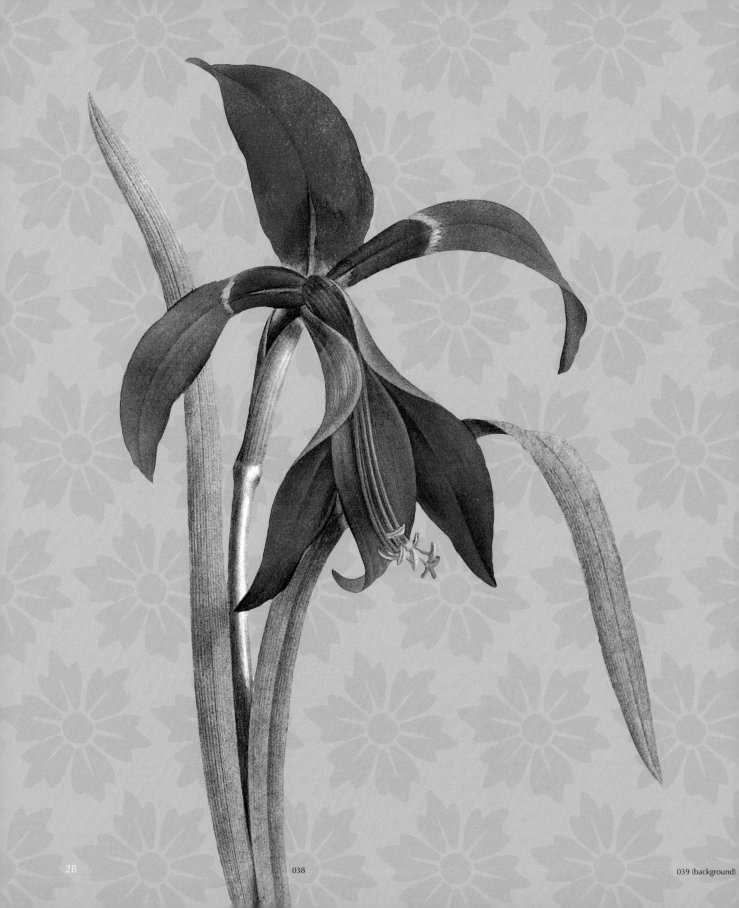

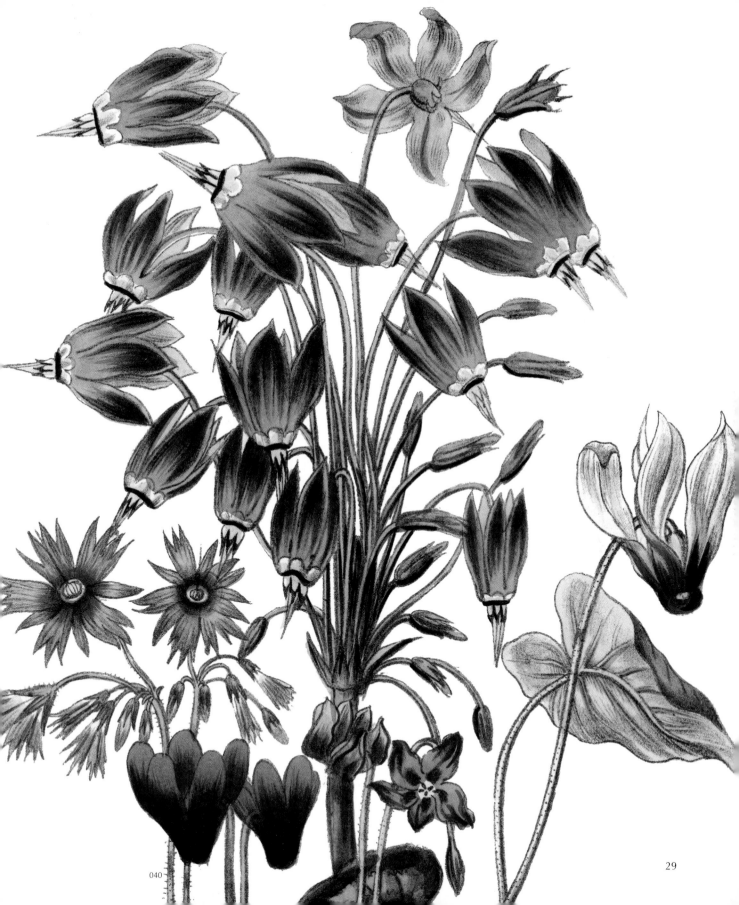

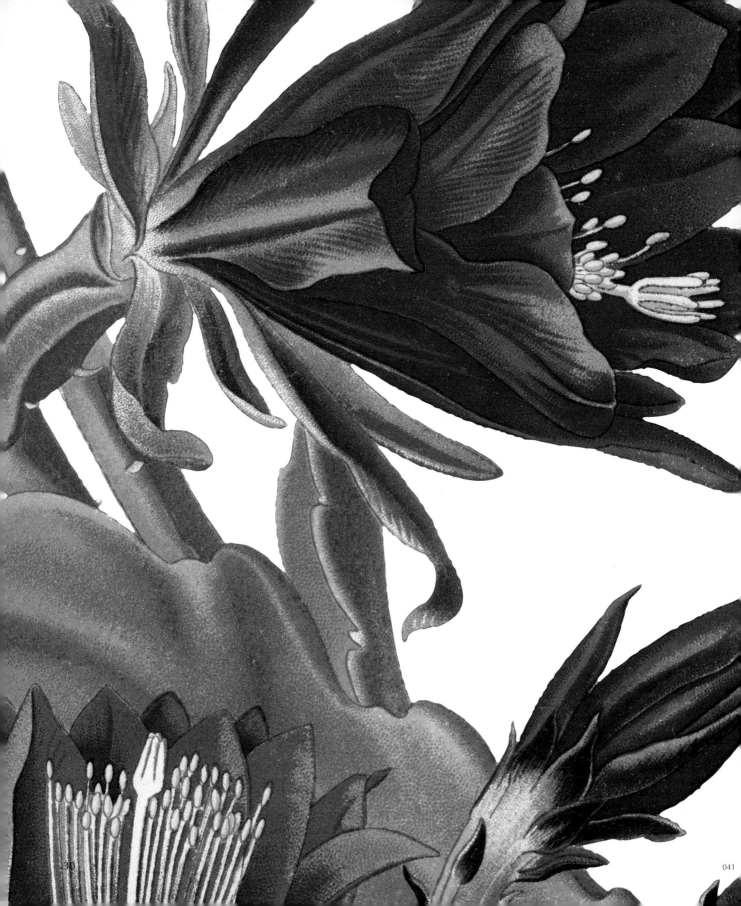

041

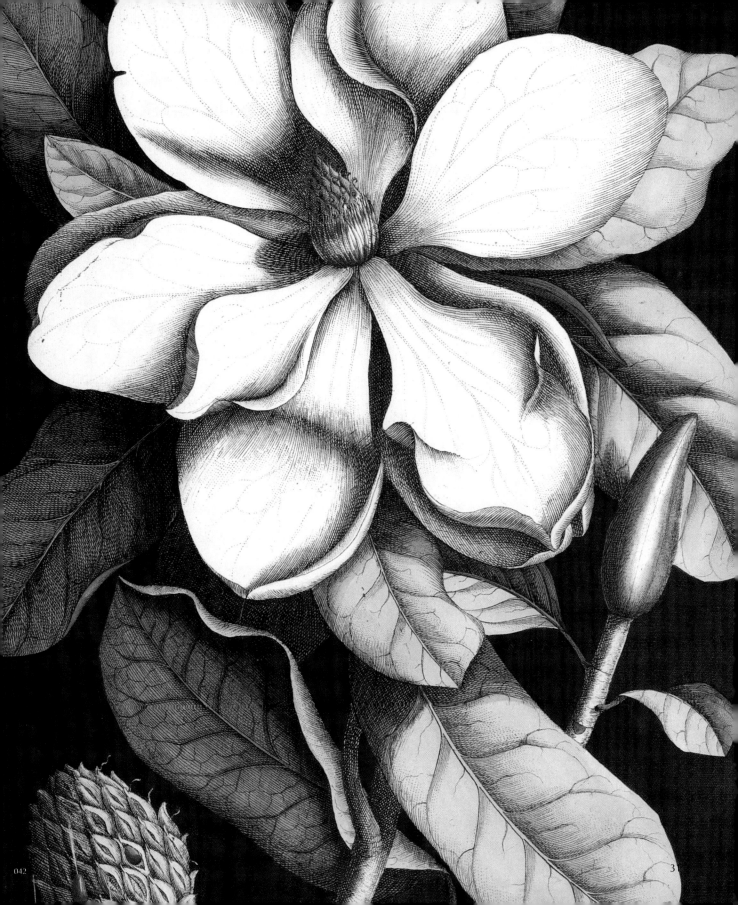

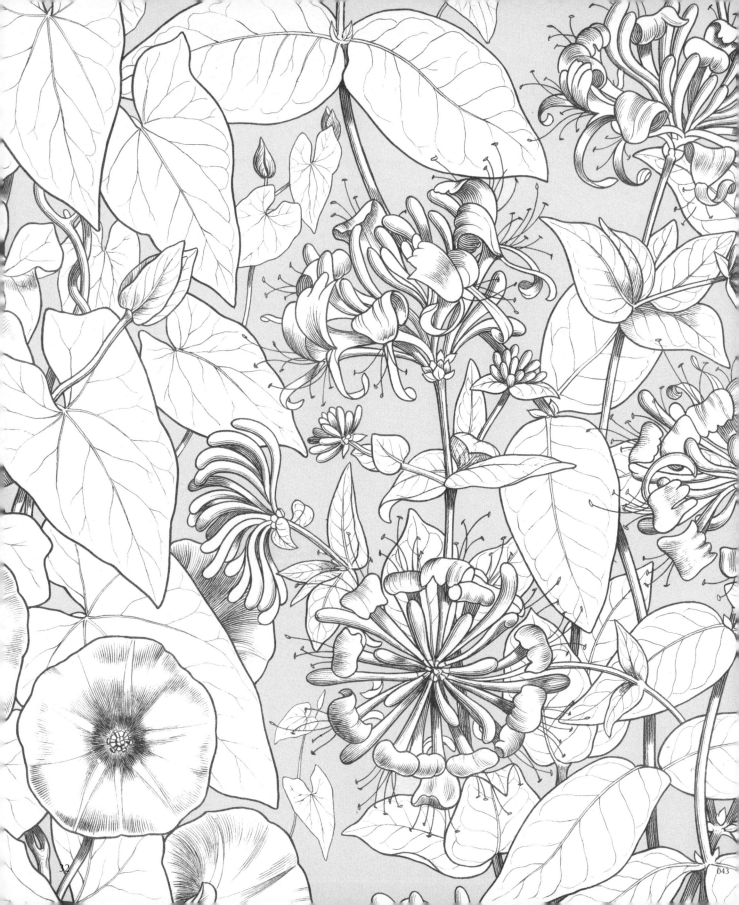

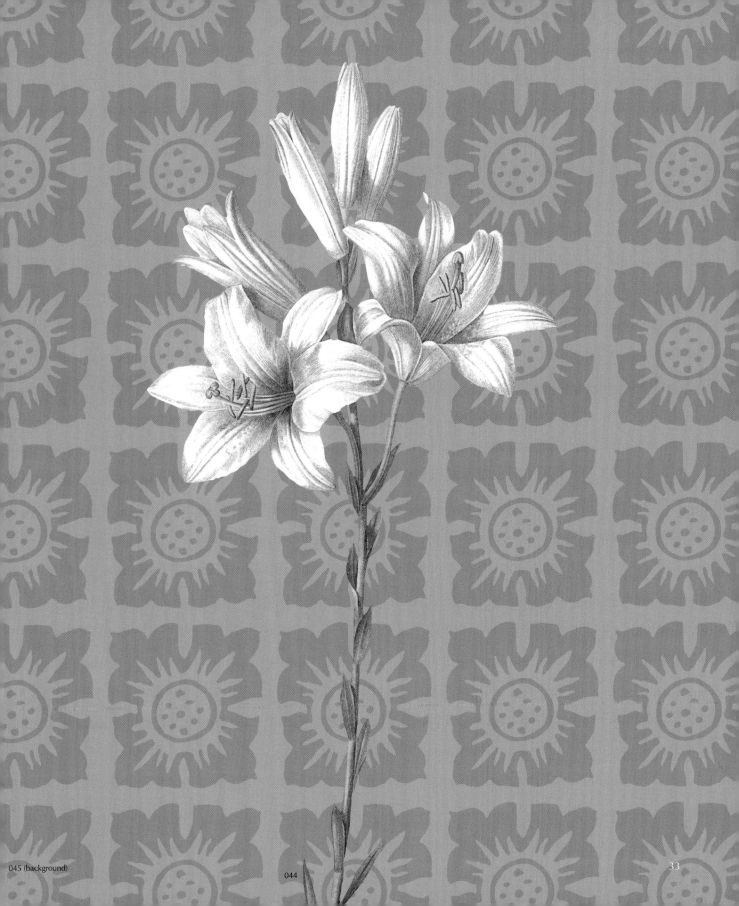

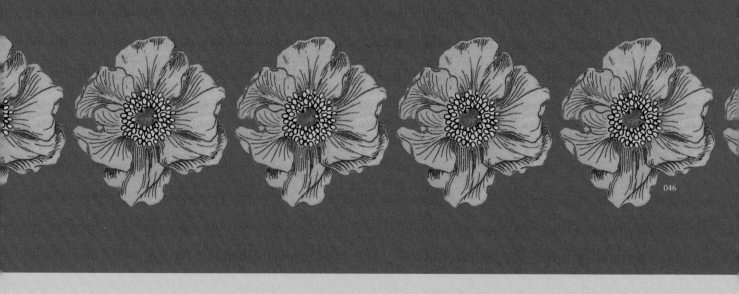

046

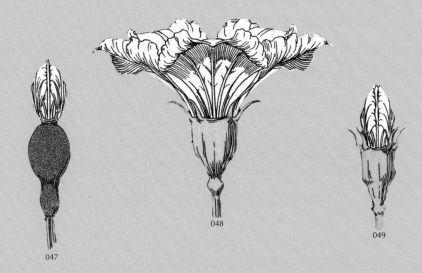

047

048

049

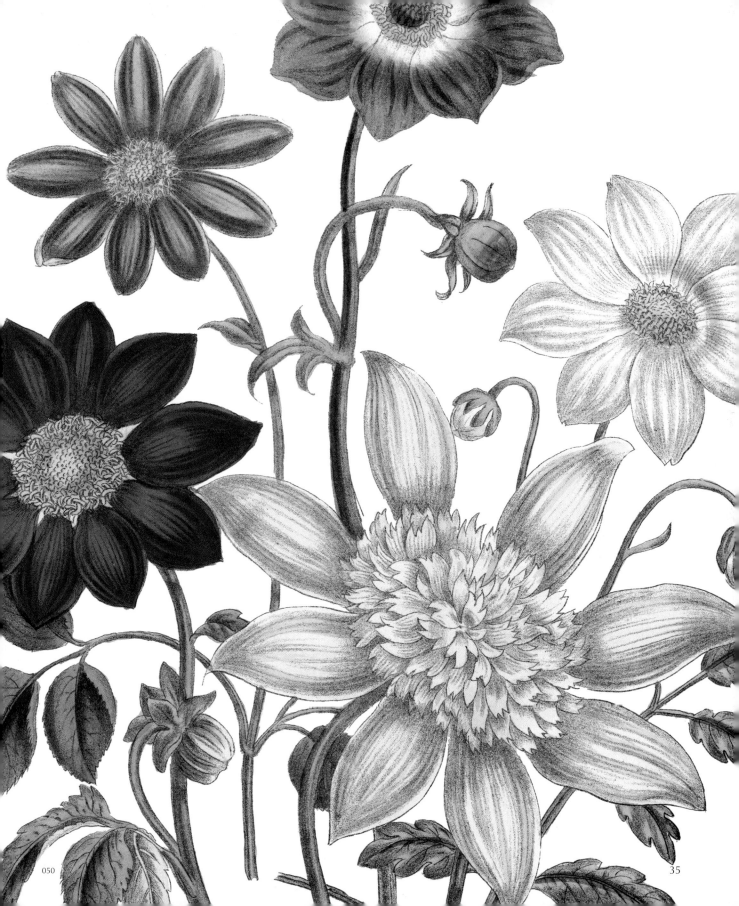

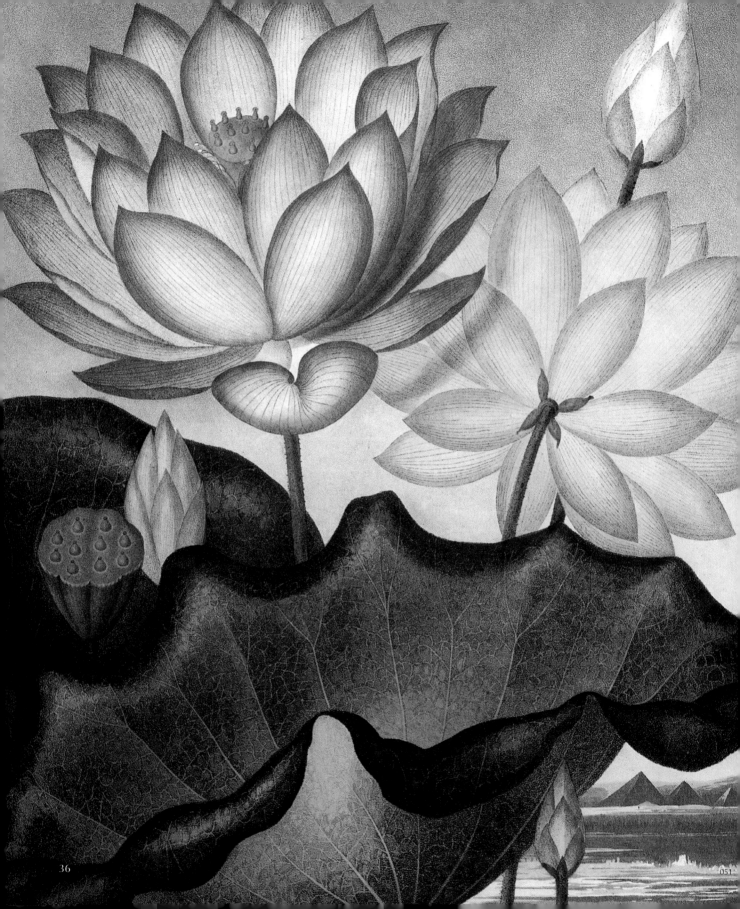

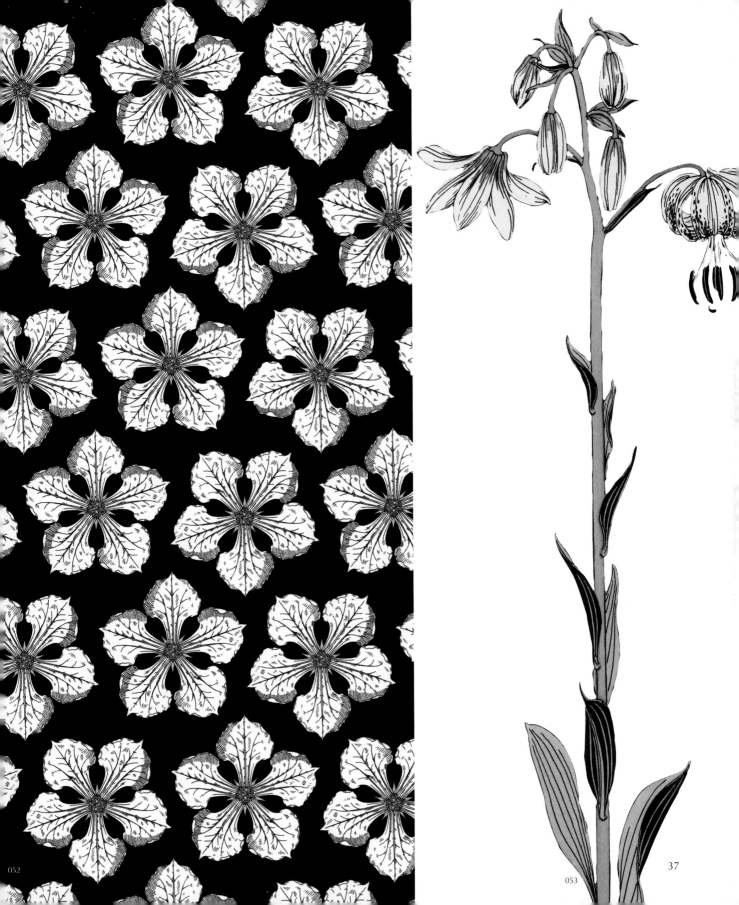

052

37

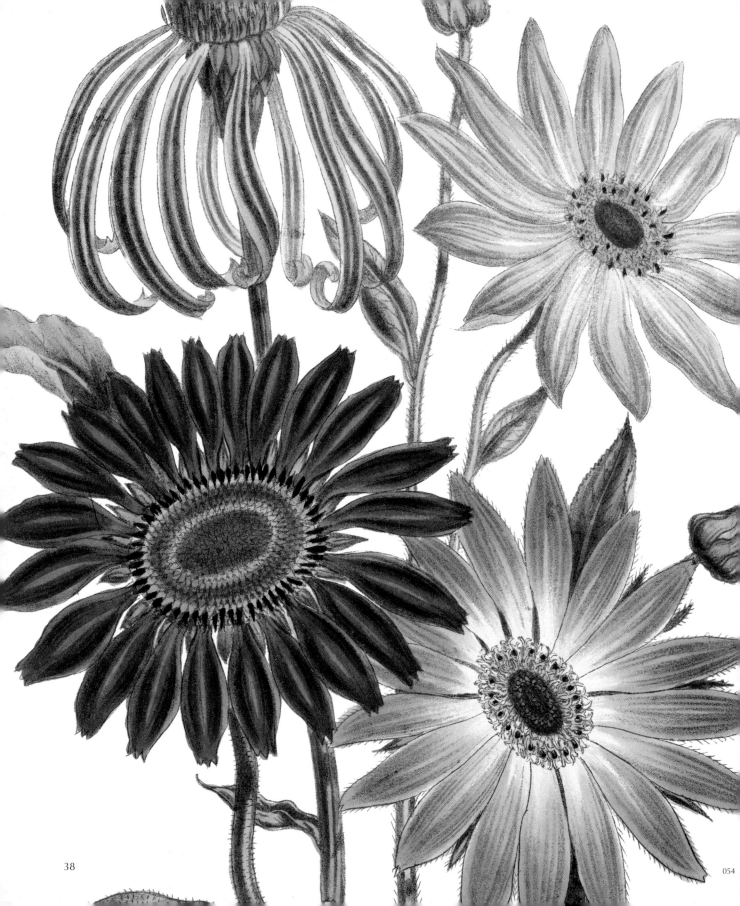

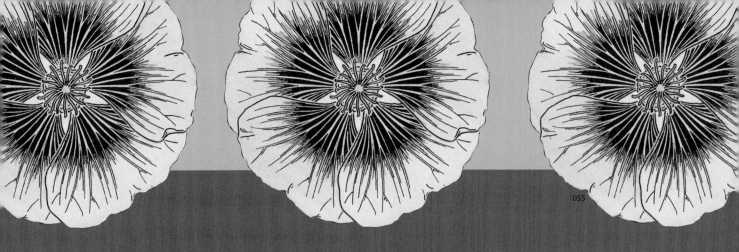

055

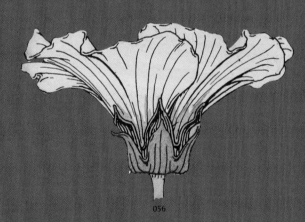

056

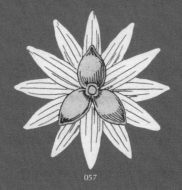

057

058

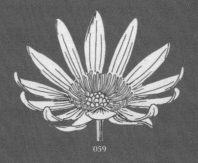

059

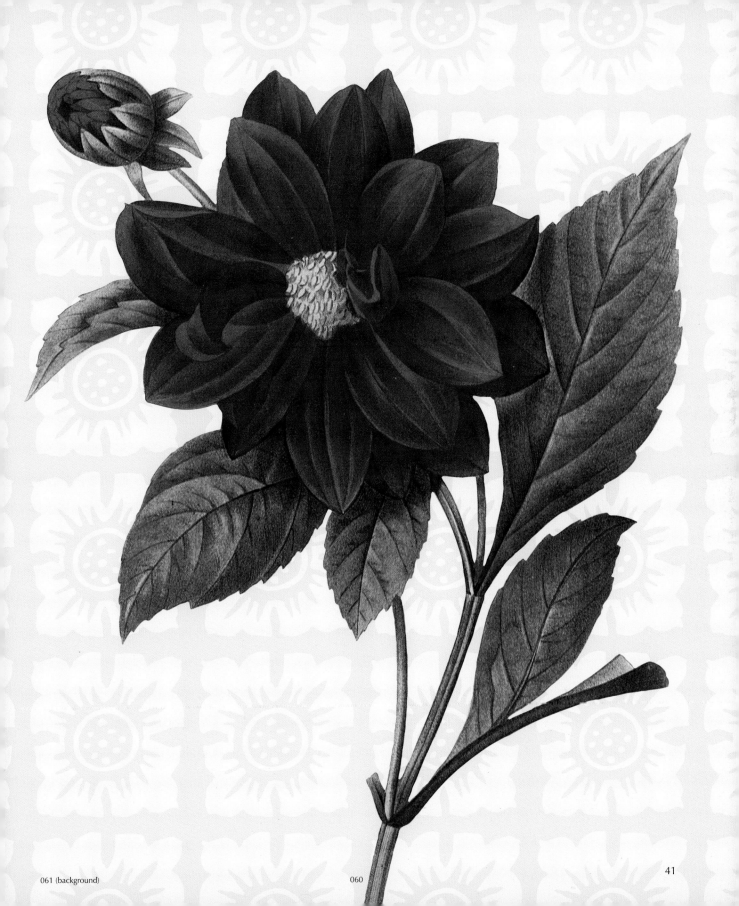

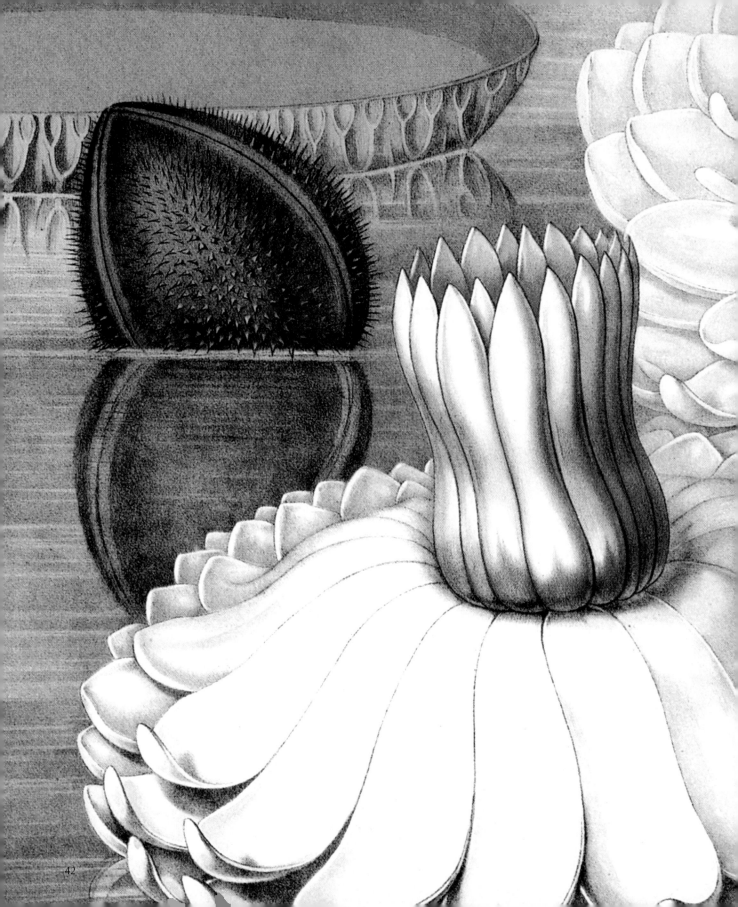

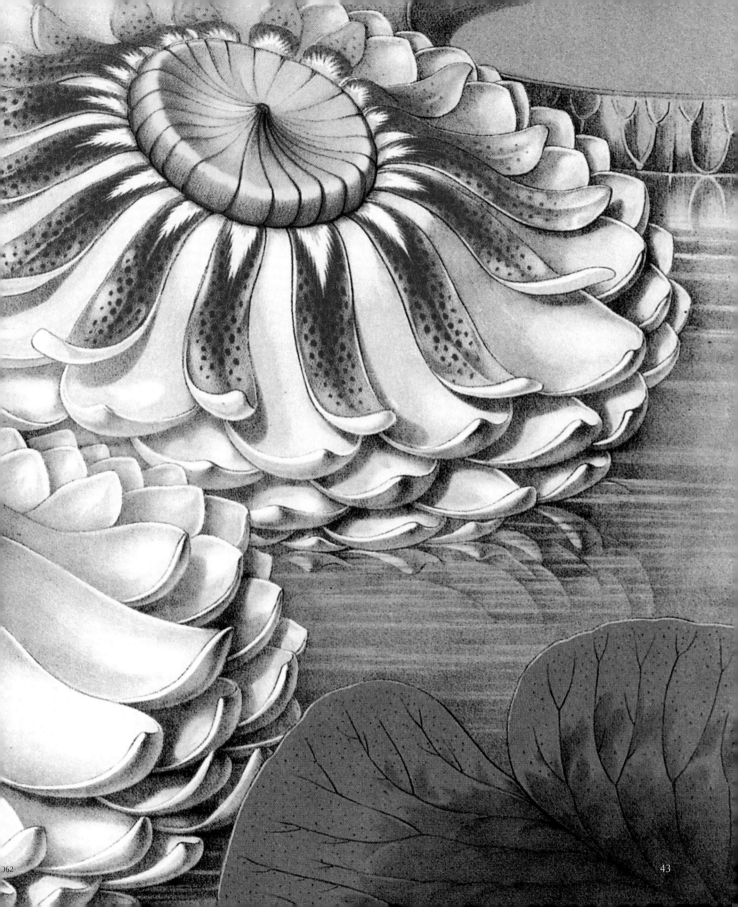

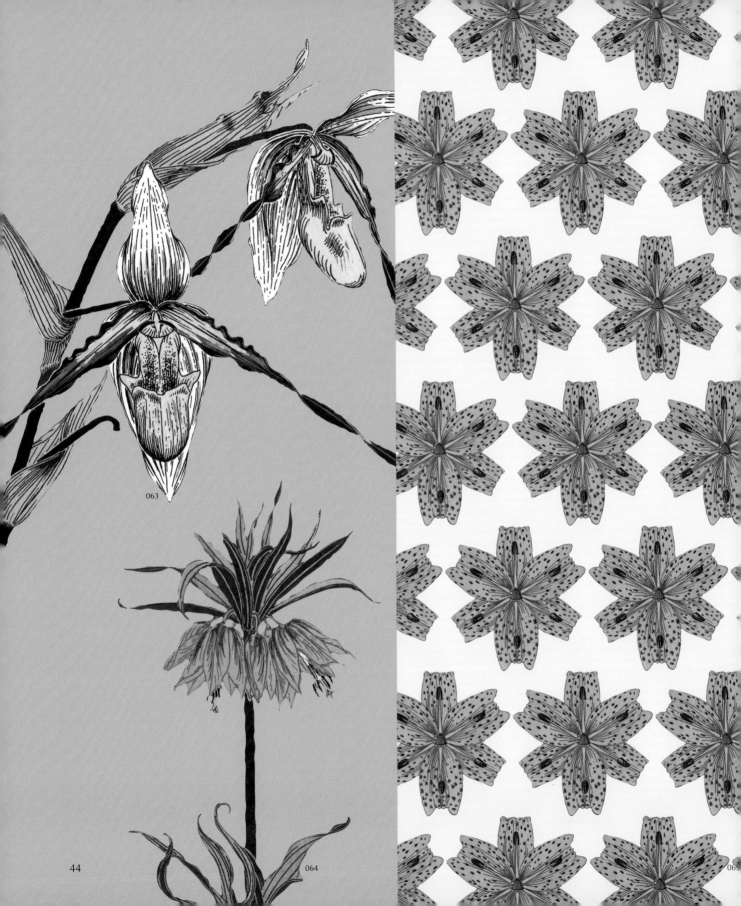

063

064

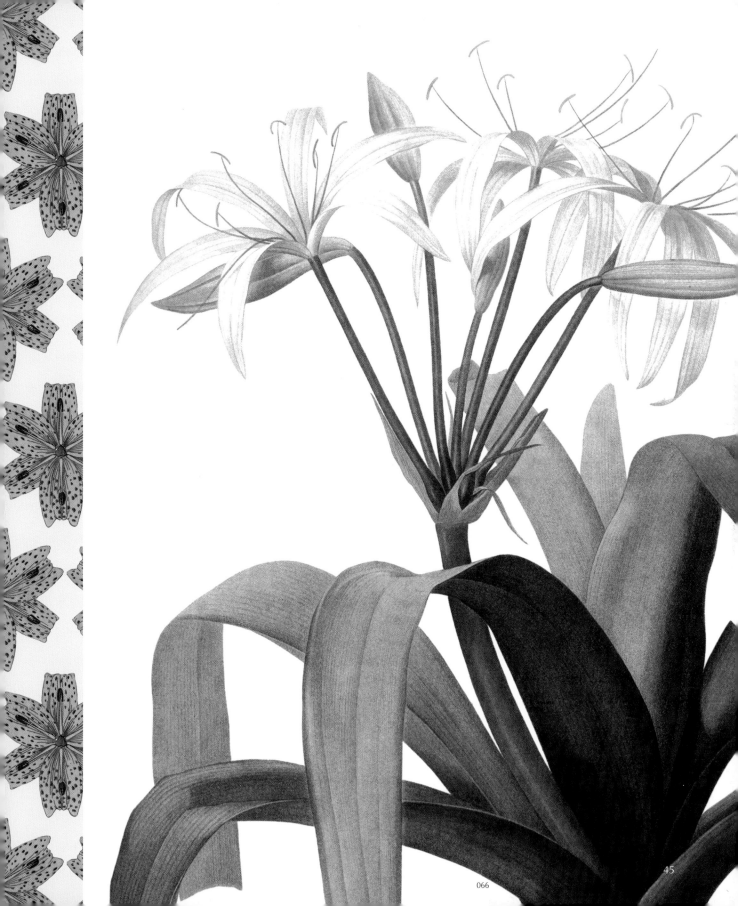

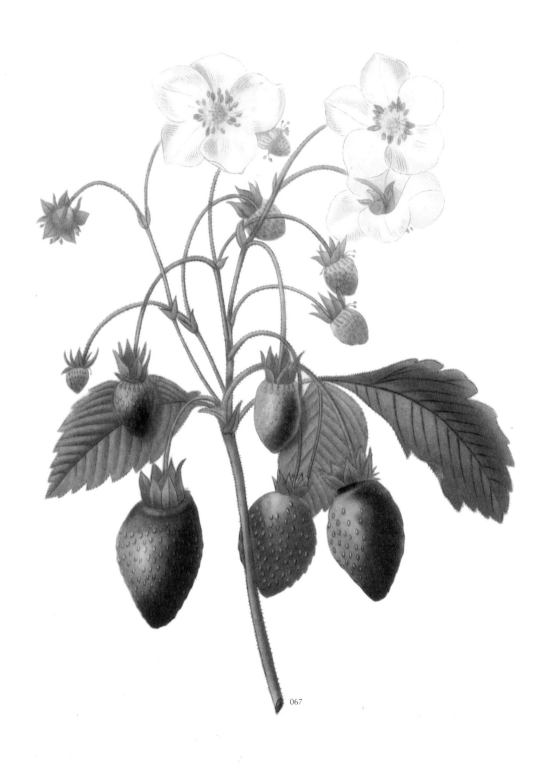

067

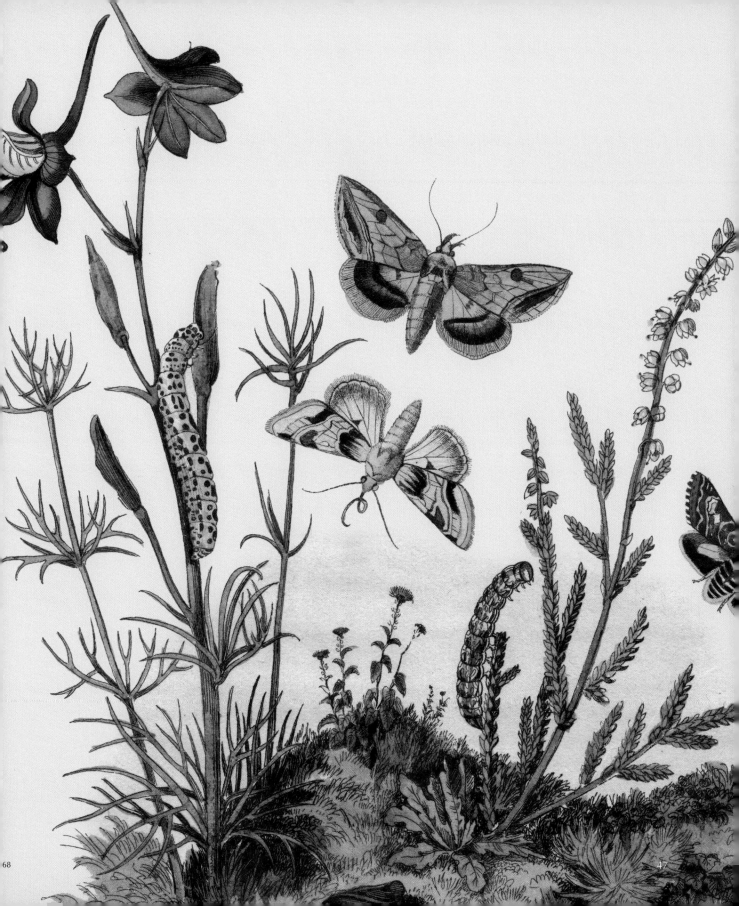

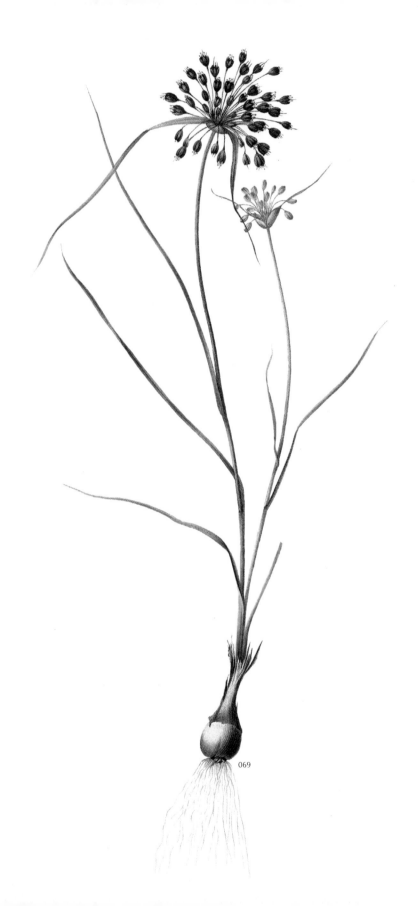

069

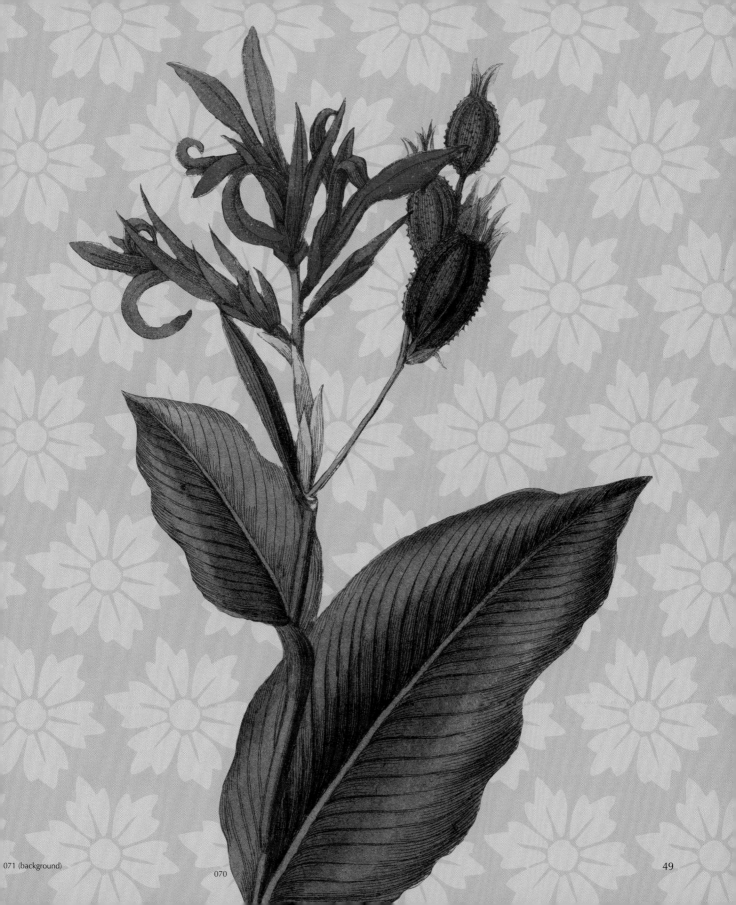

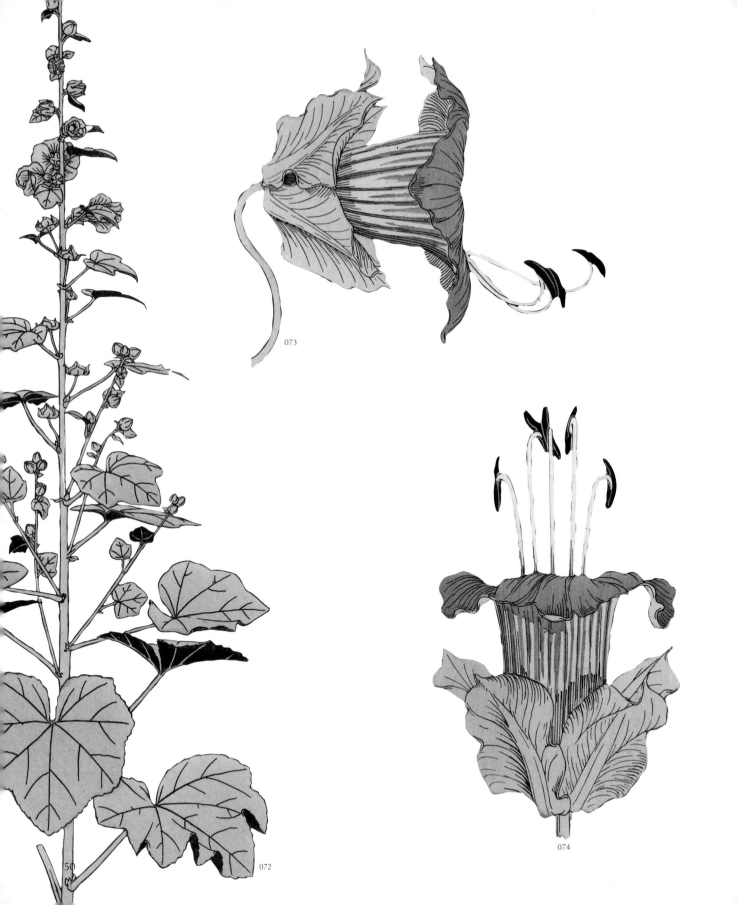

50

072

073

074

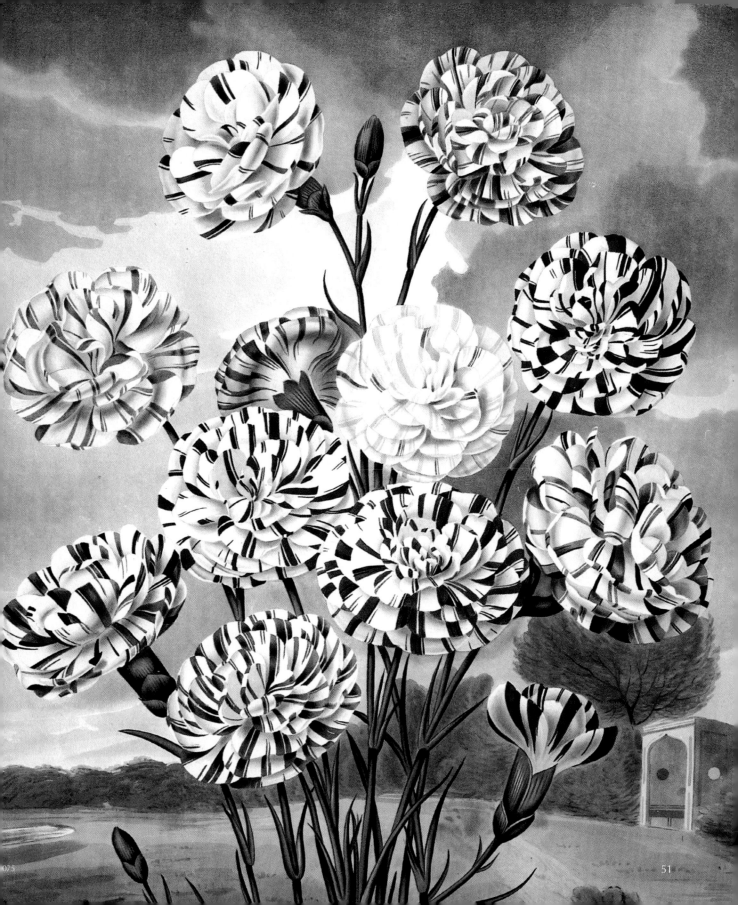

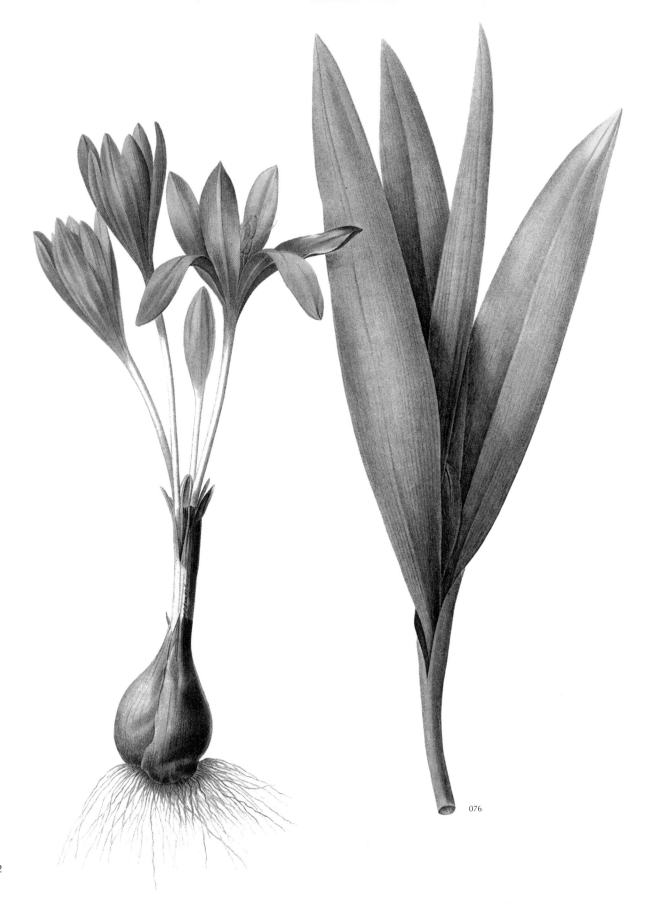

52

076

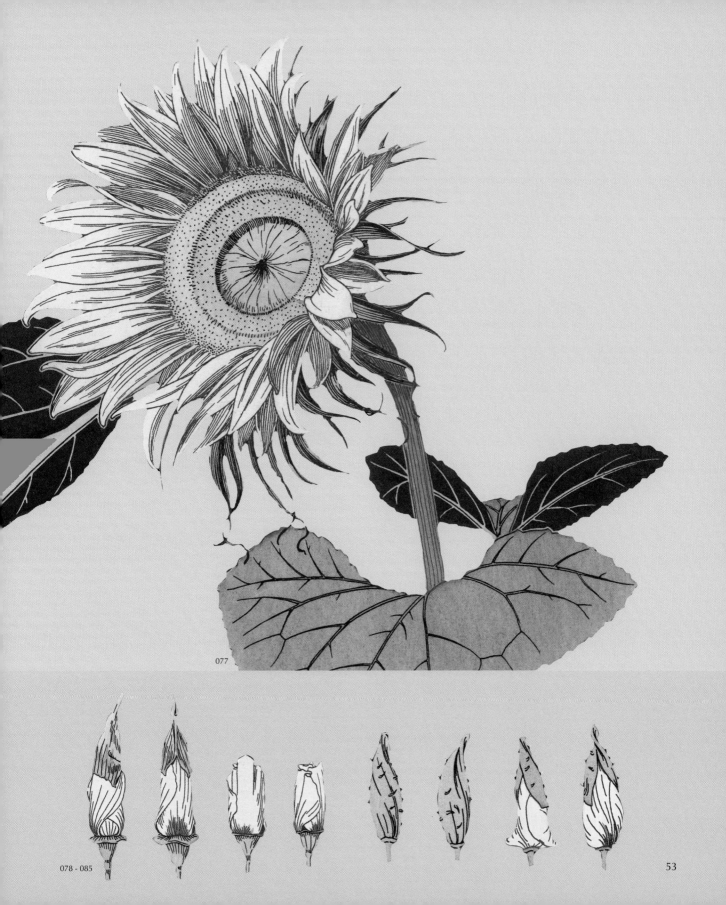

077

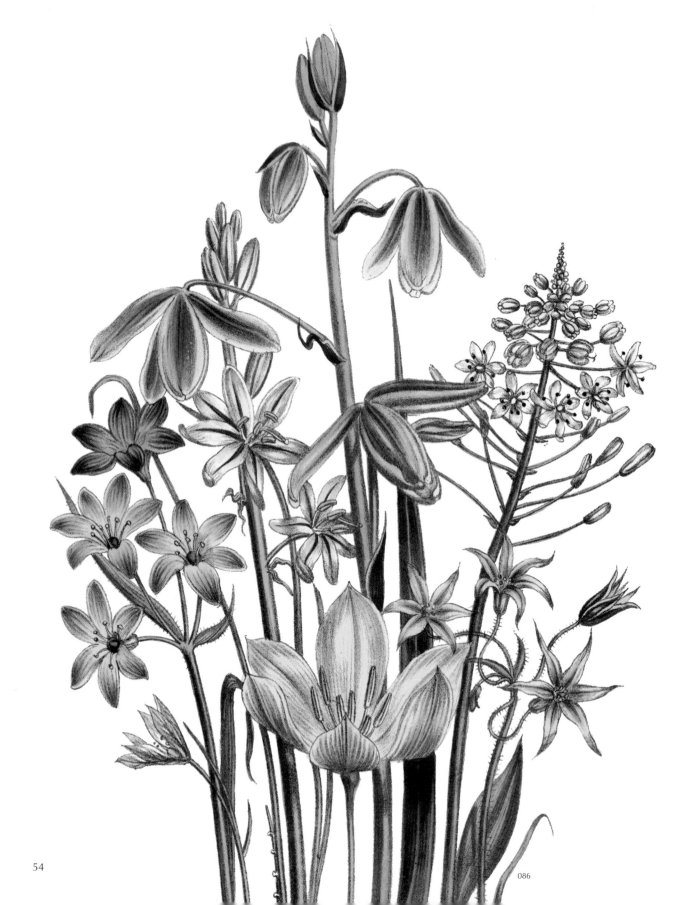

086

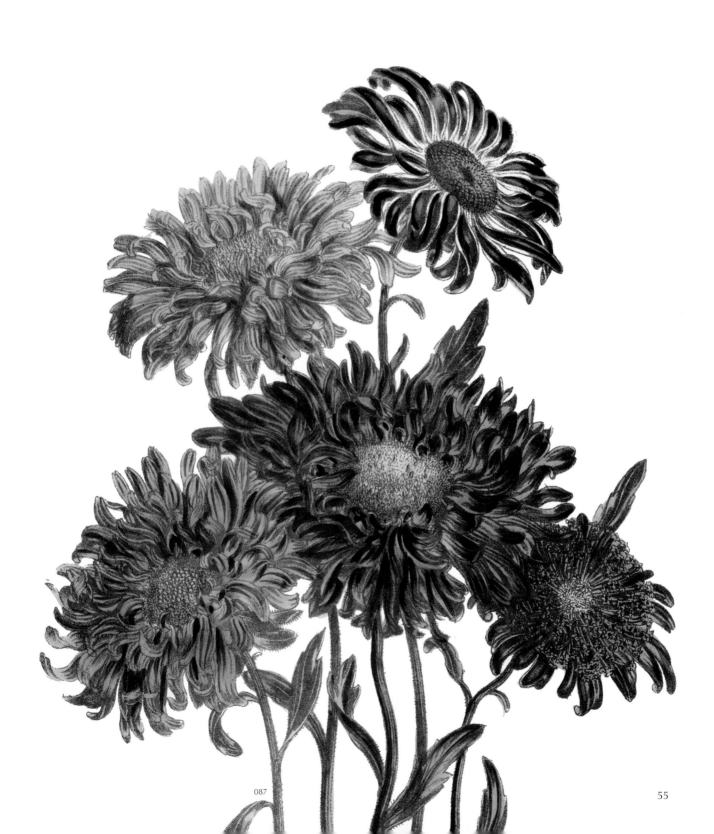

087

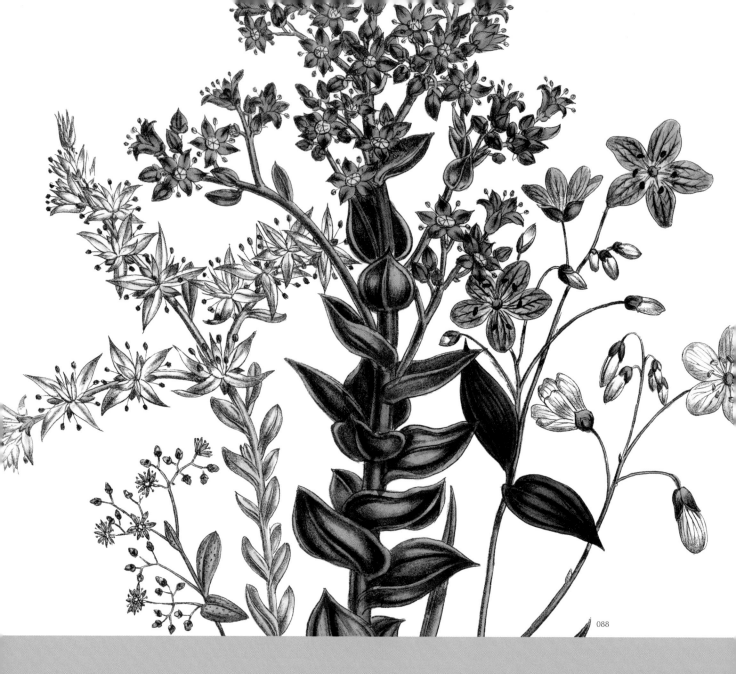

088

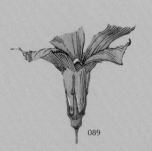

089

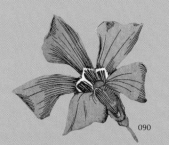

090

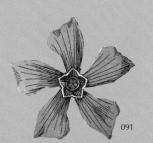

091

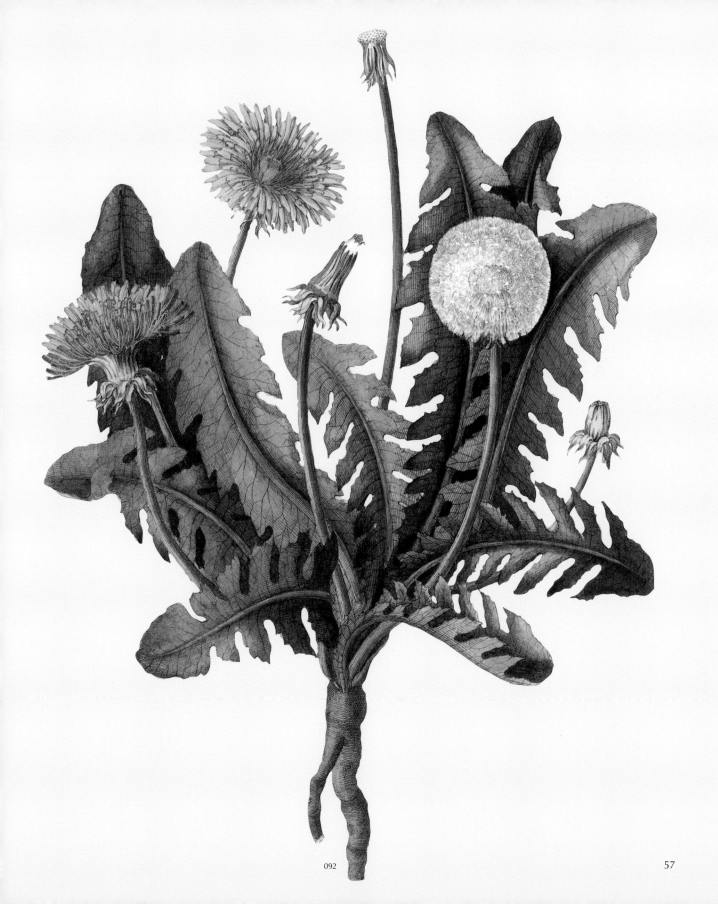

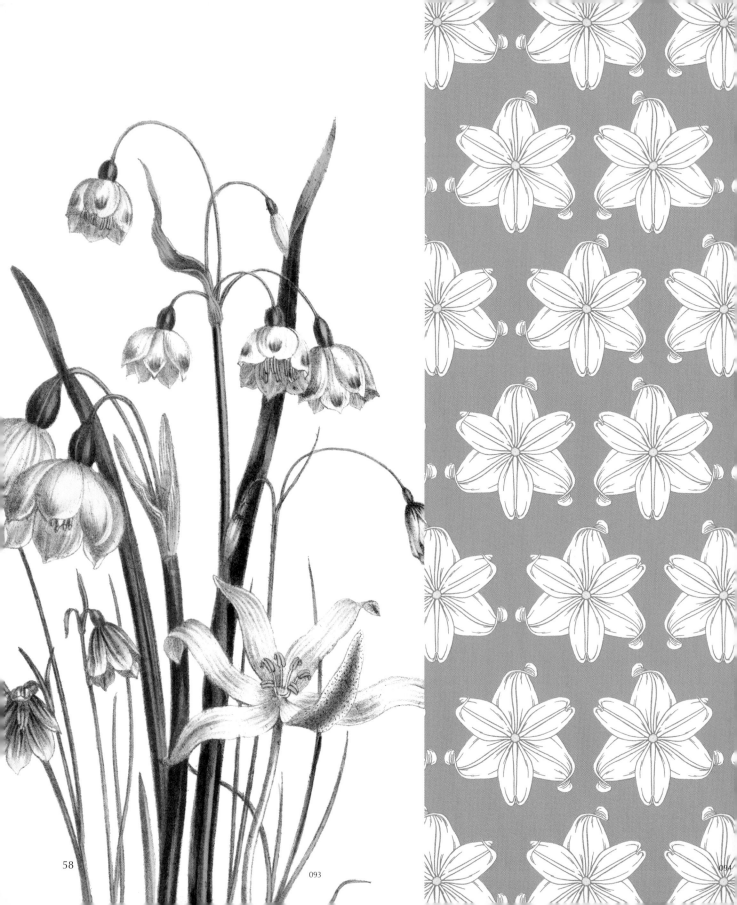

093

094

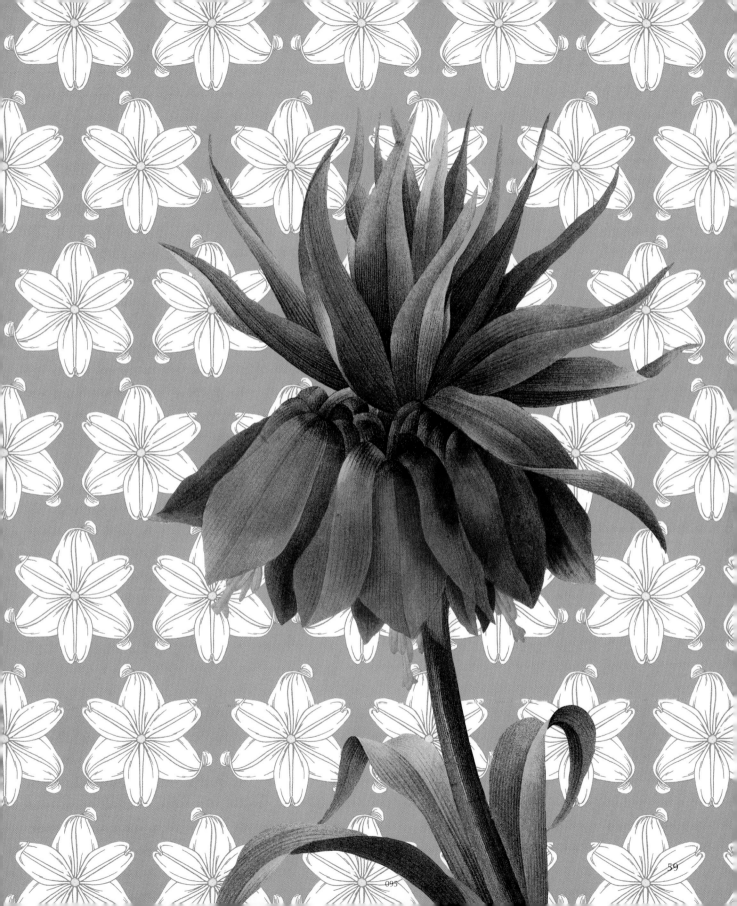

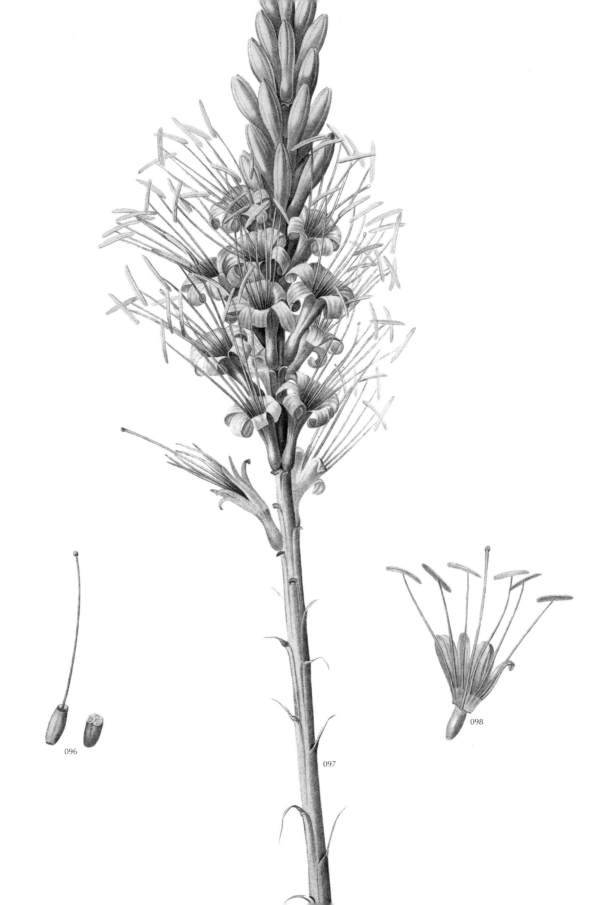

096

097

098

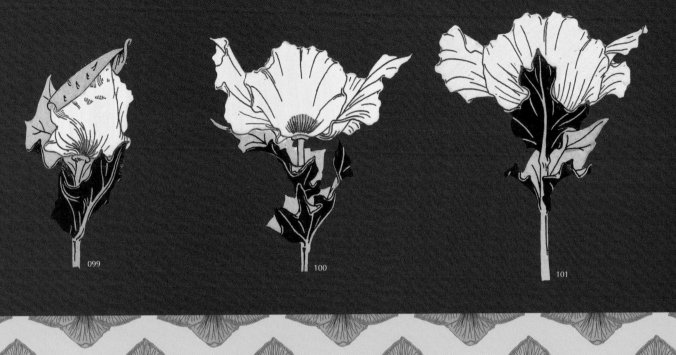

099

100

101

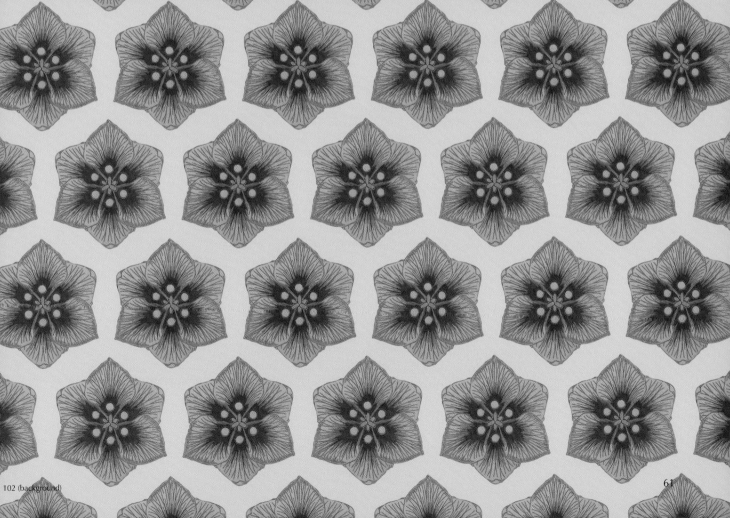

102 (background)

61

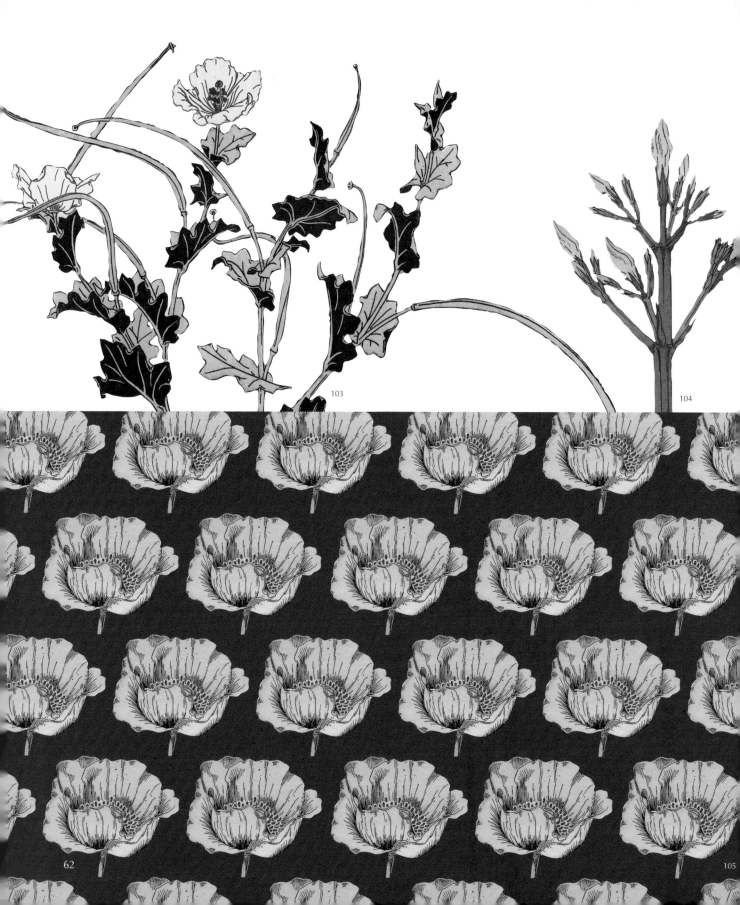

103

104

105

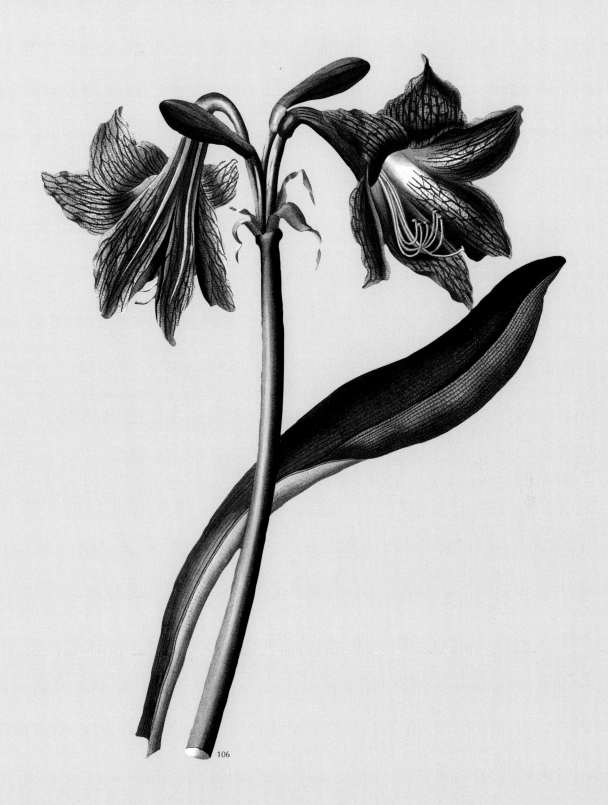

106

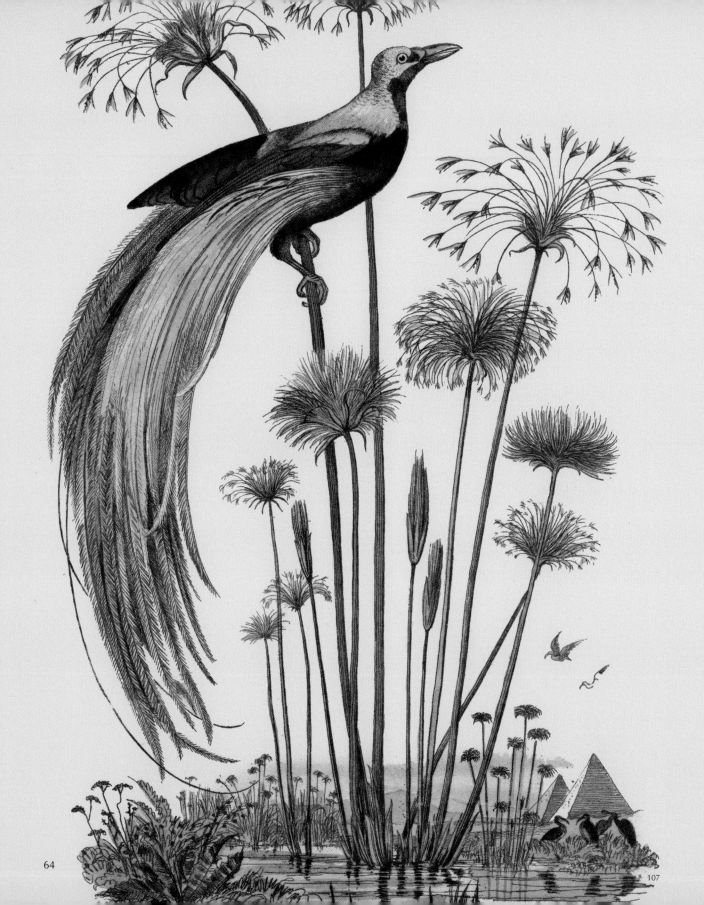

107

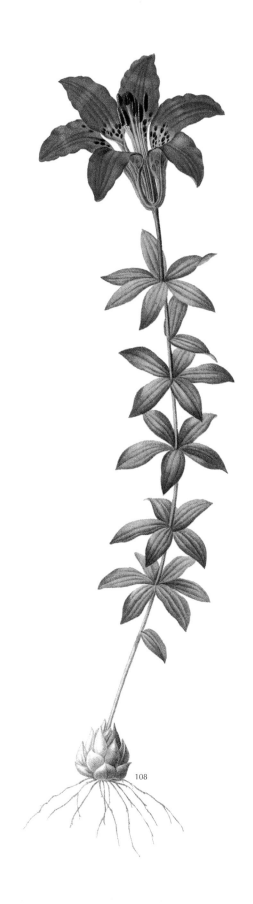

108

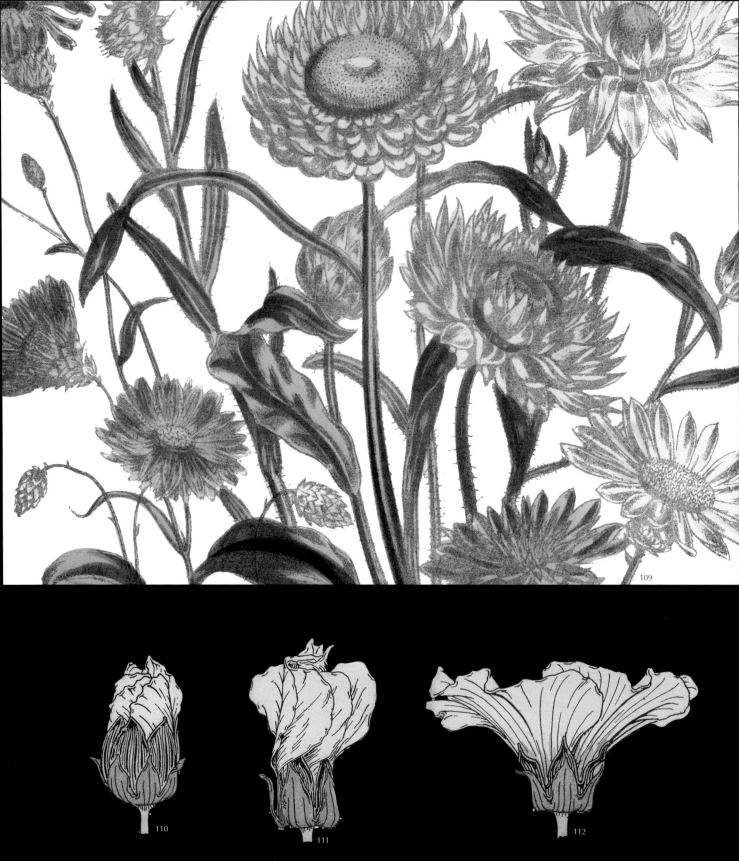

109

110

111

112

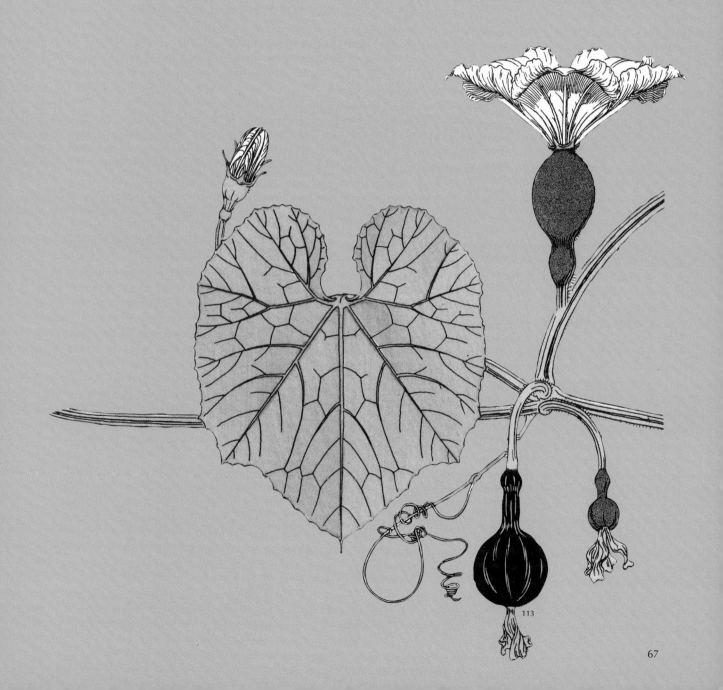

113

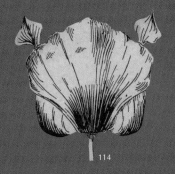

114

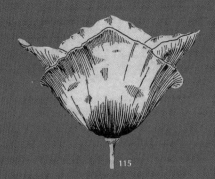

115

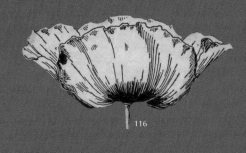

116

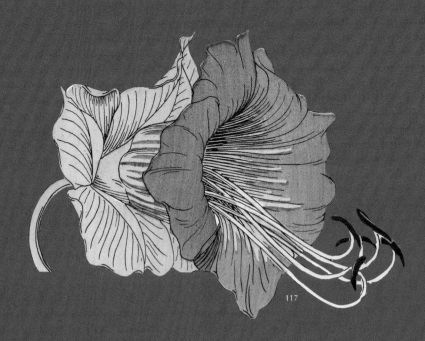

117

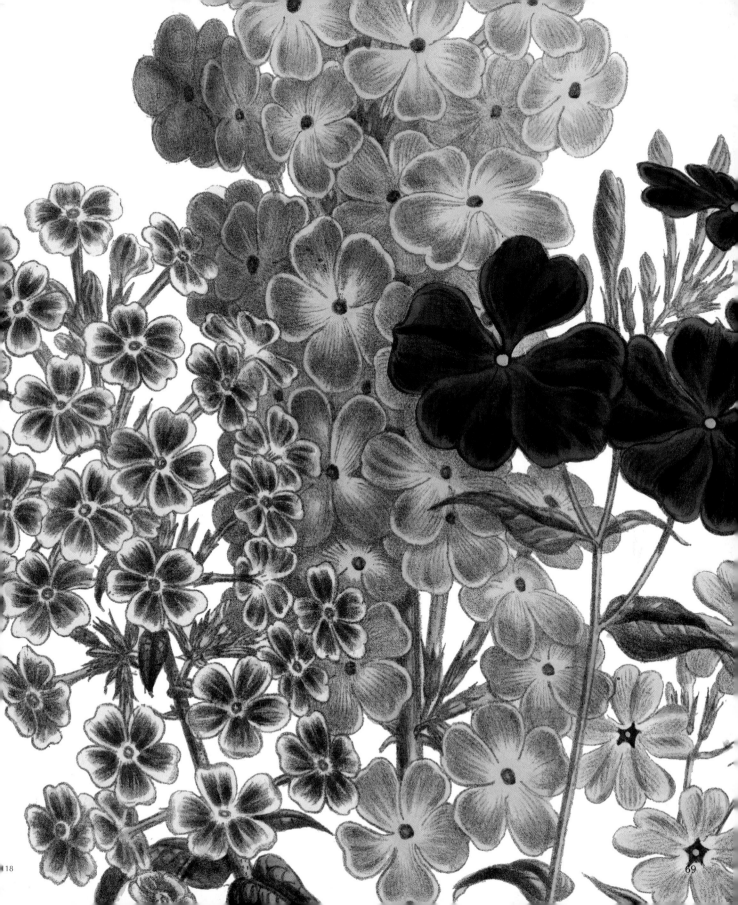

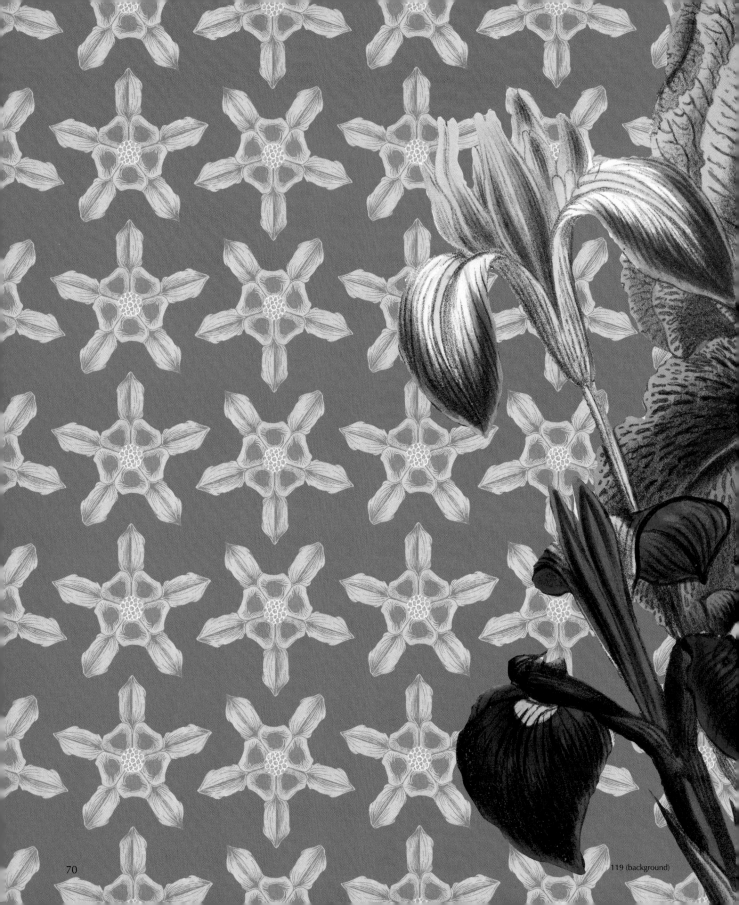

70

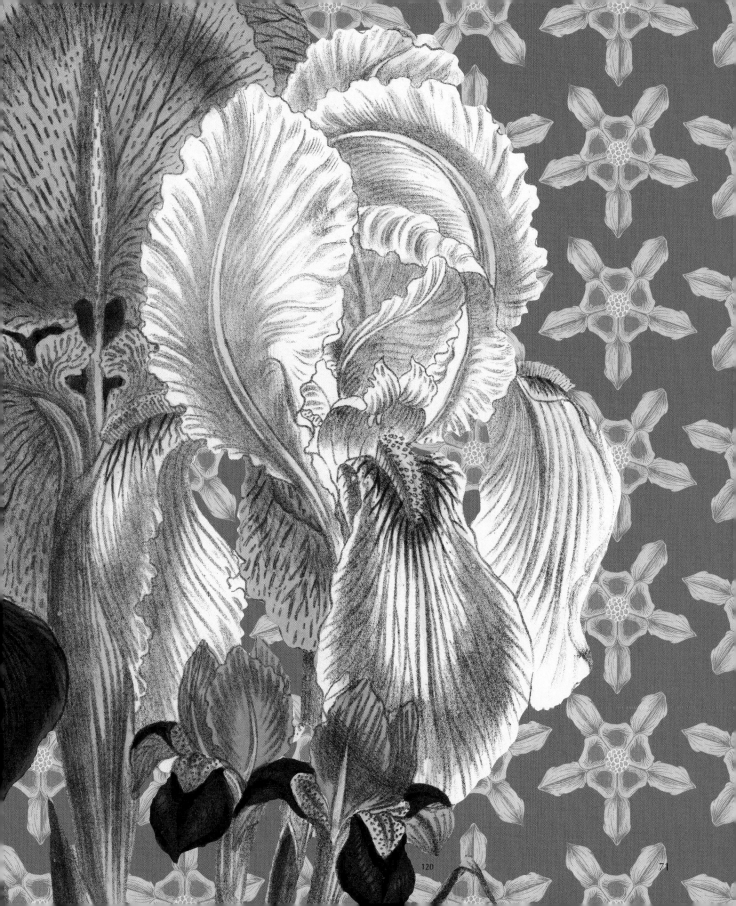

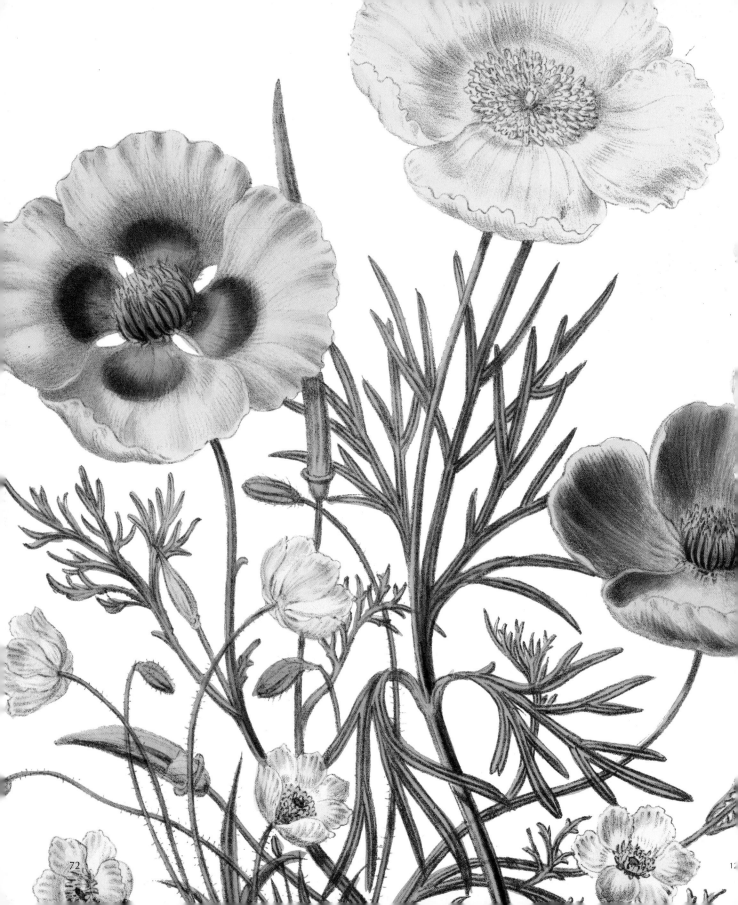

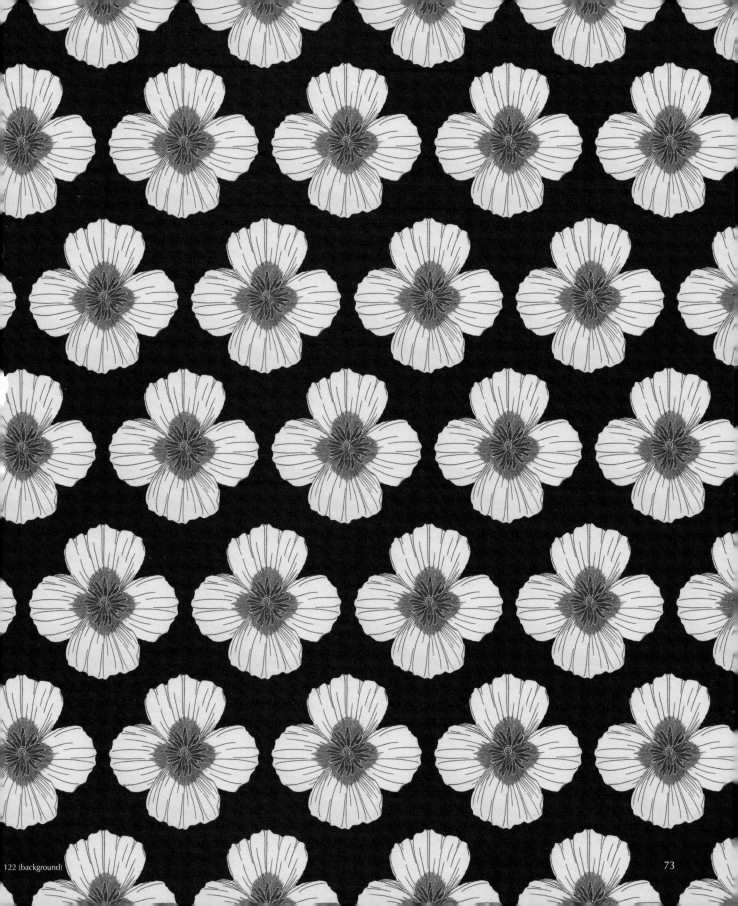

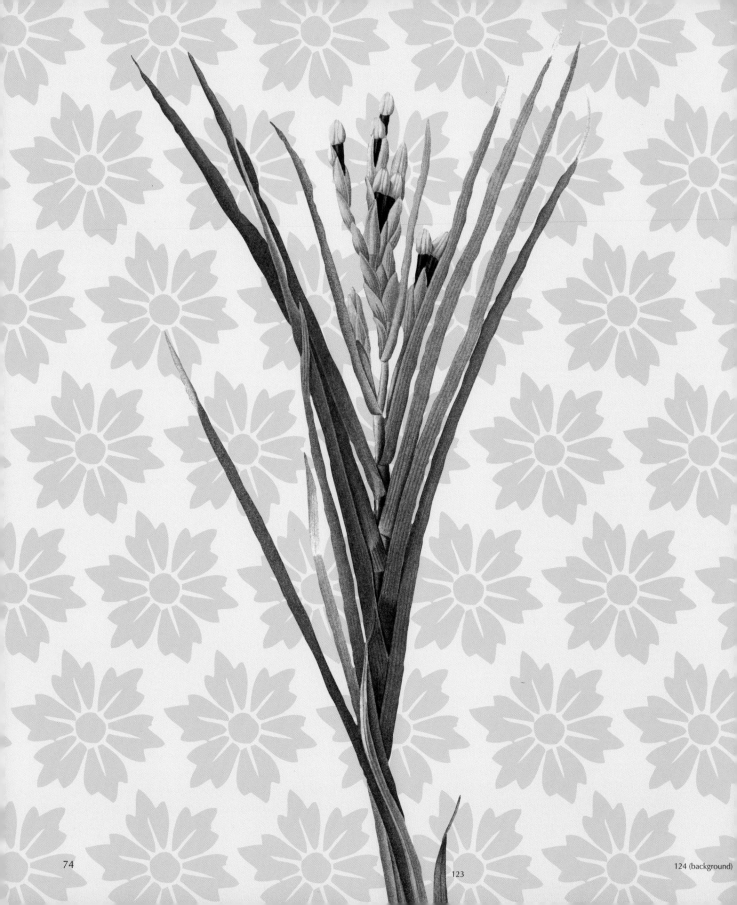

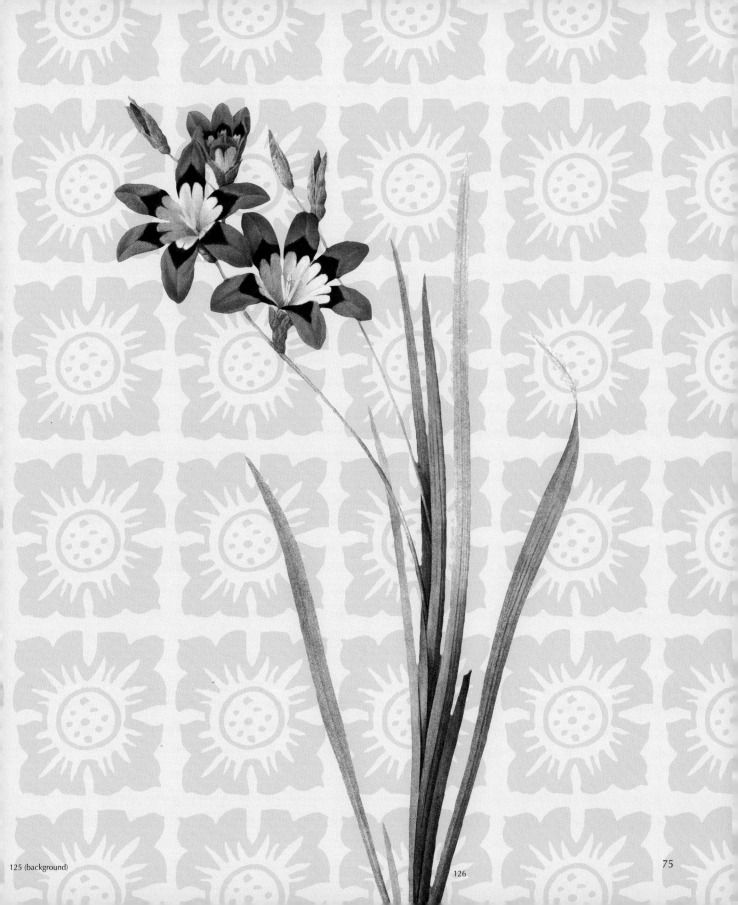

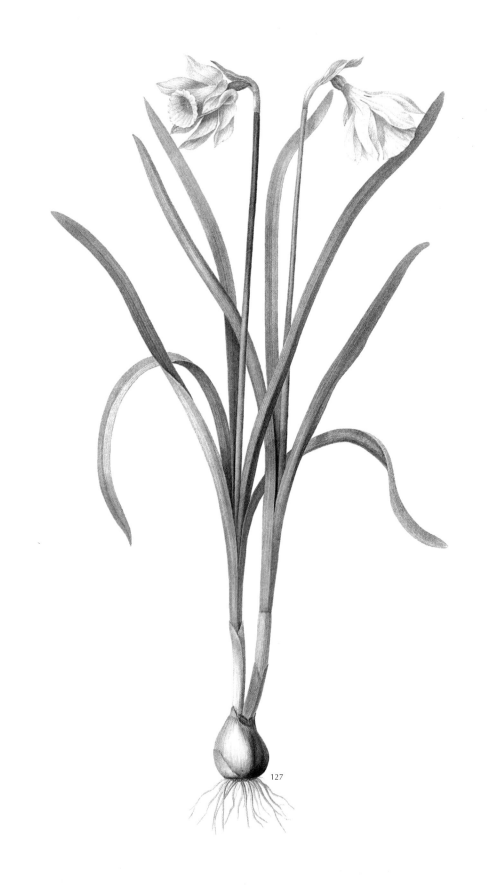

127

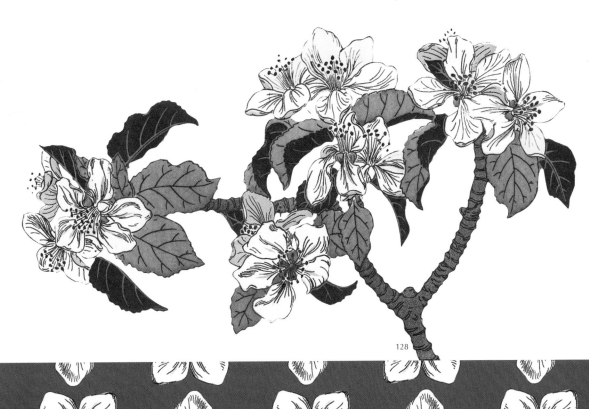

128

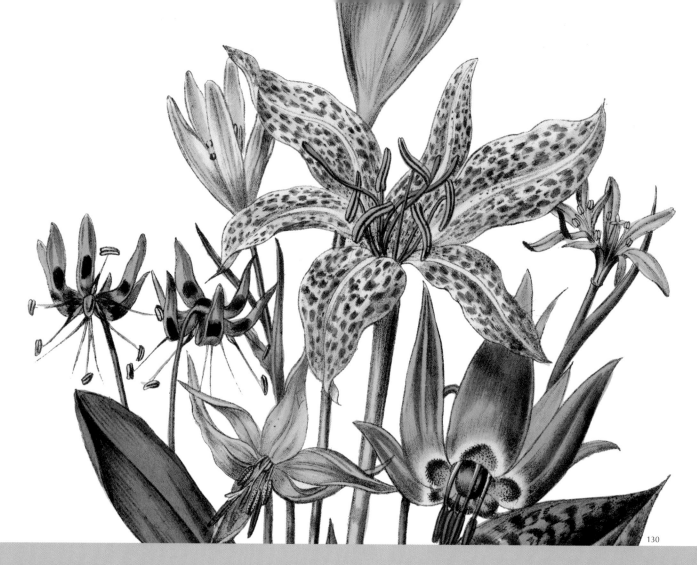

130

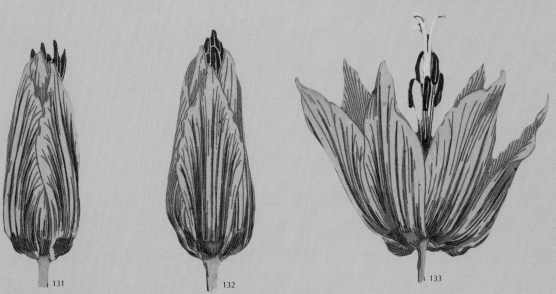

131

132

133

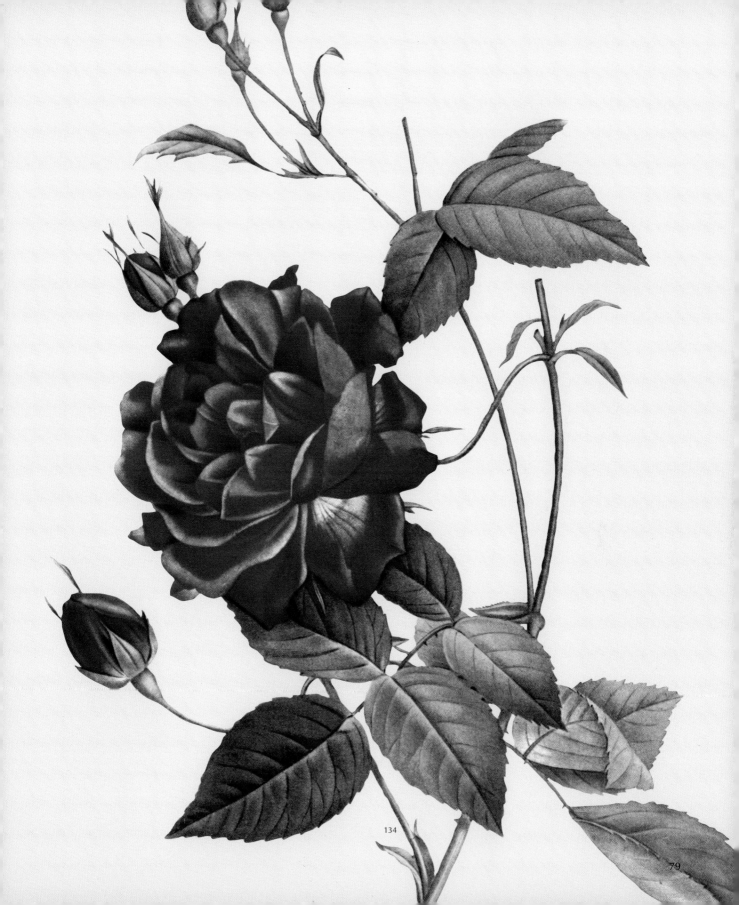

134

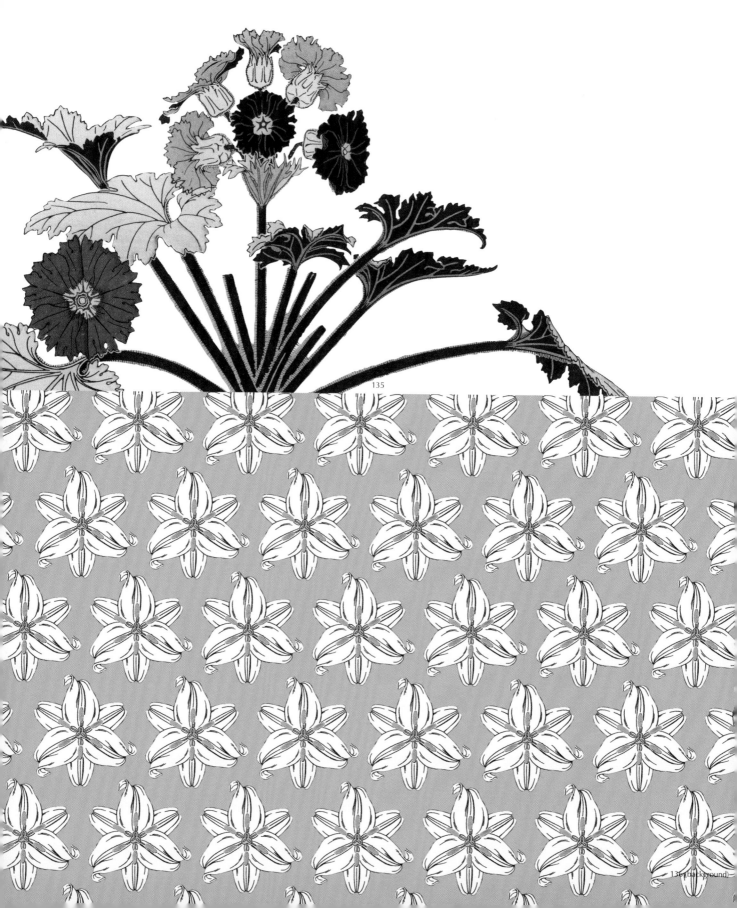

135

135 (background)

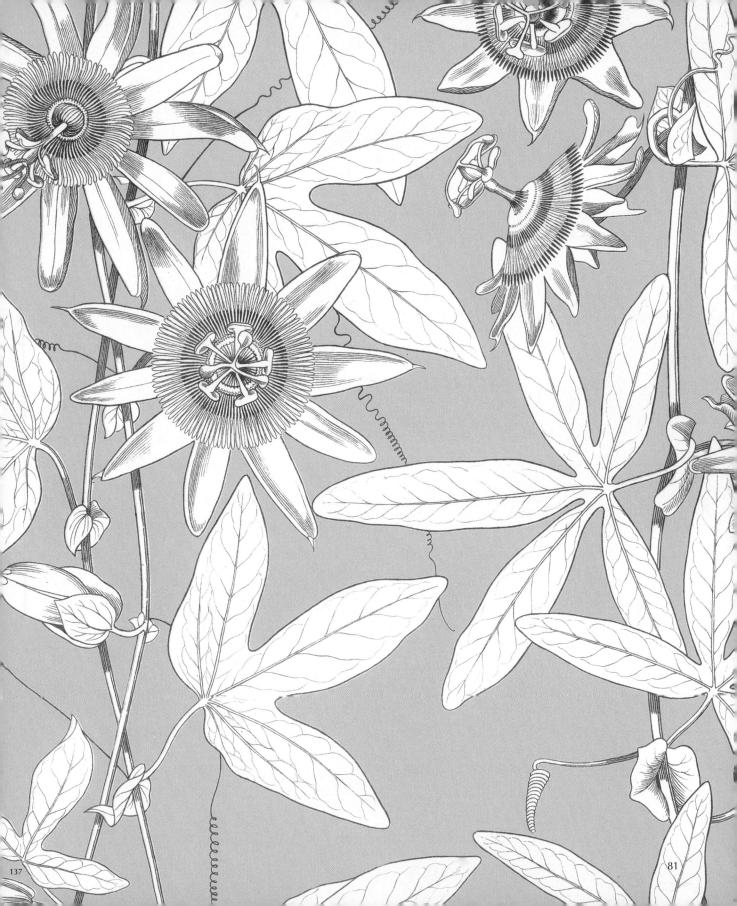

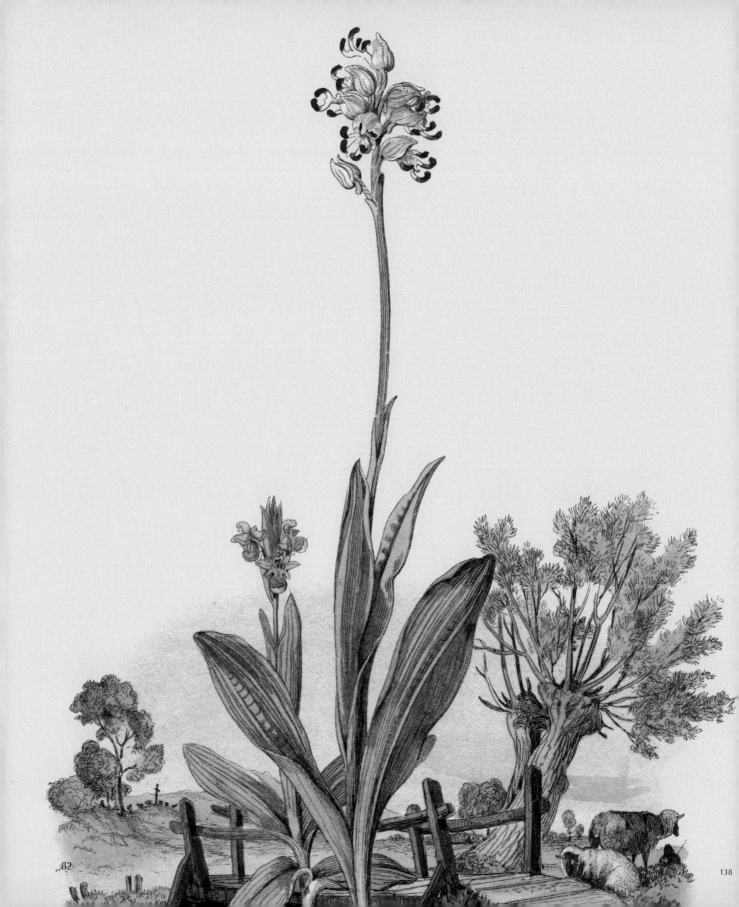

138

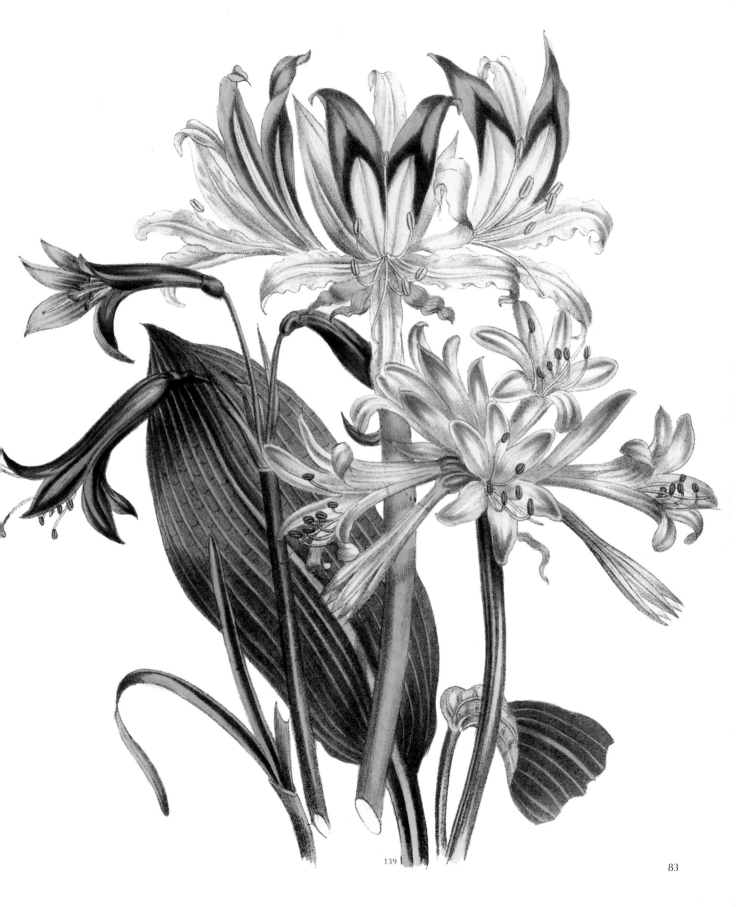

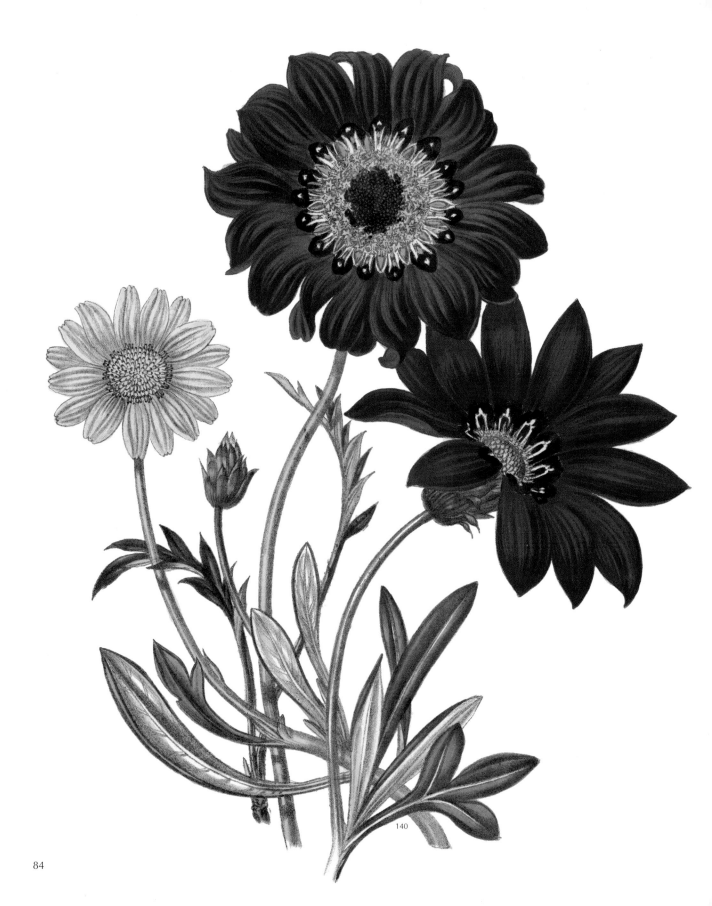

140

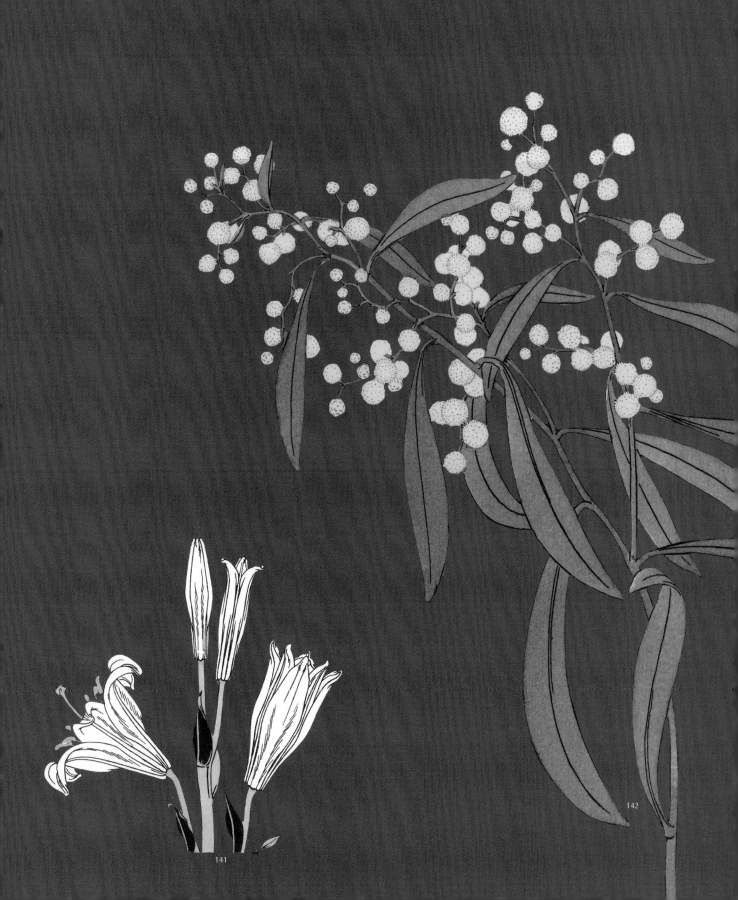

141

142

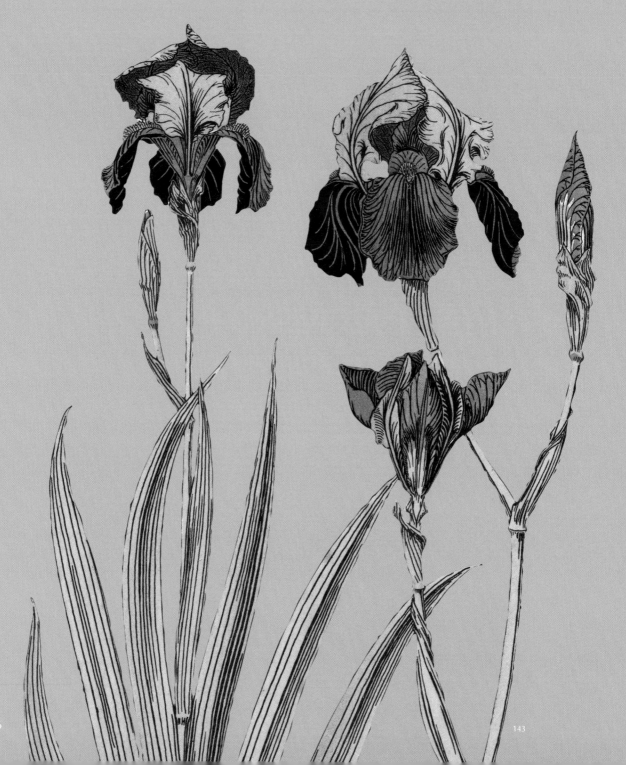

143

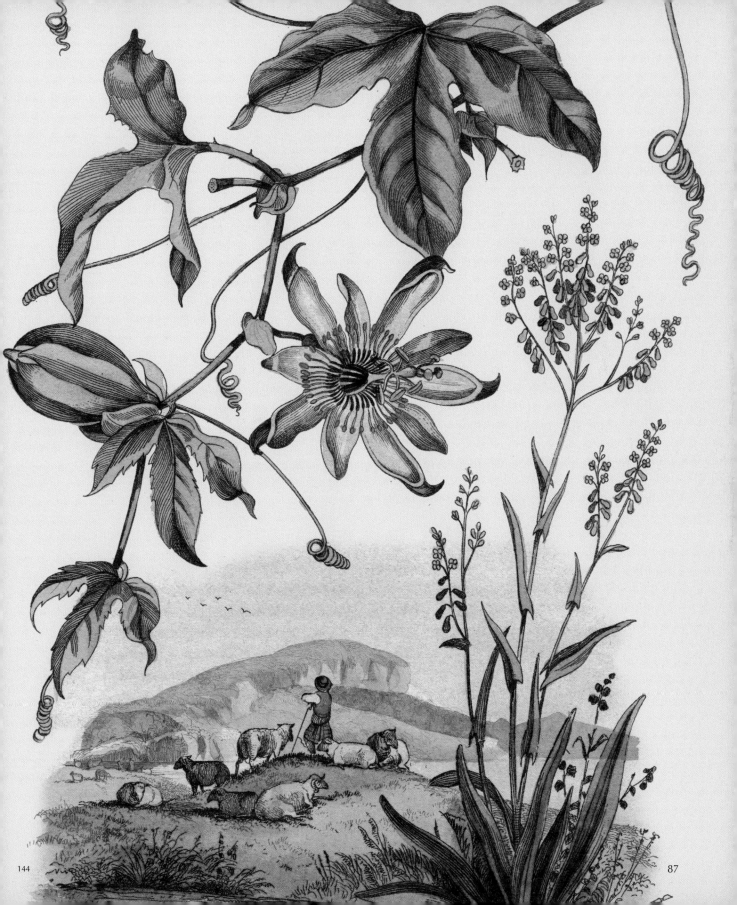

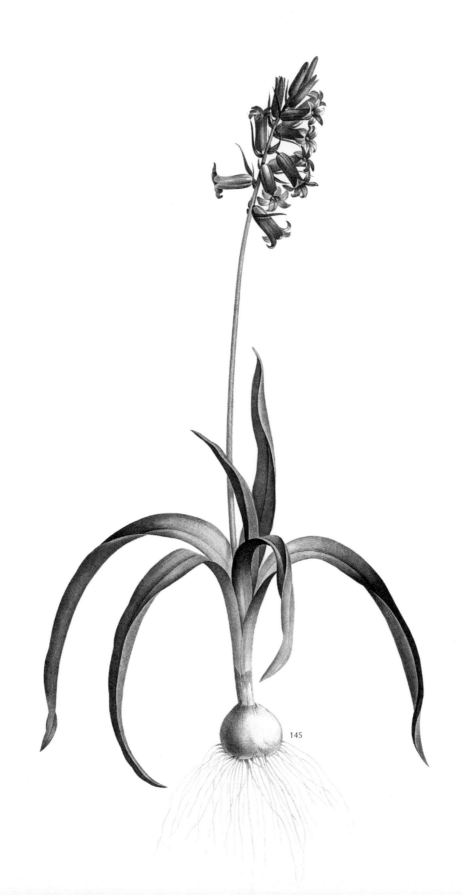

145

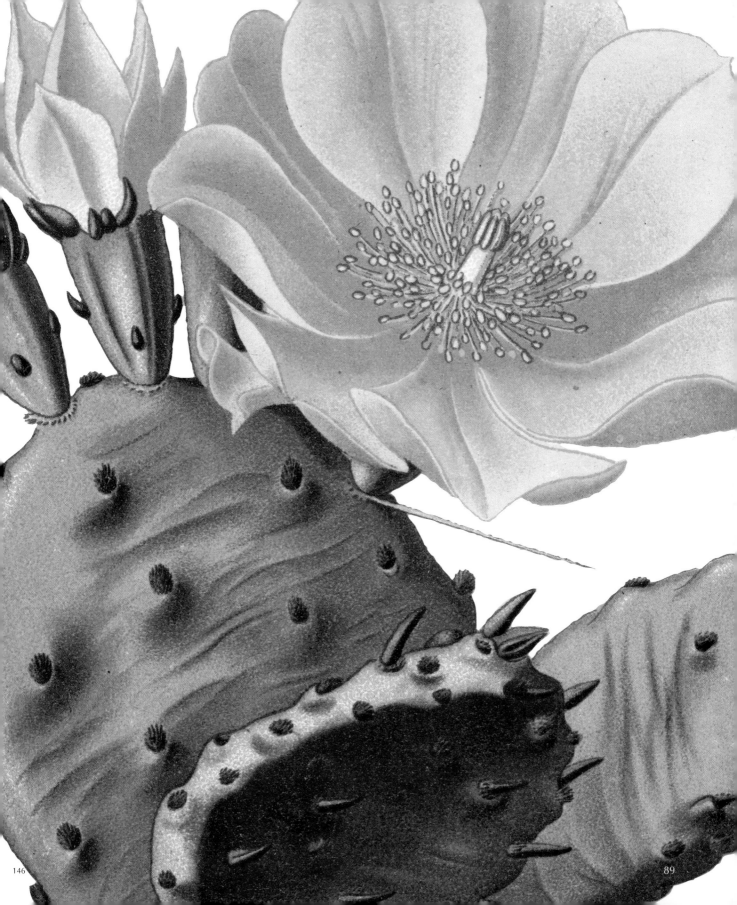

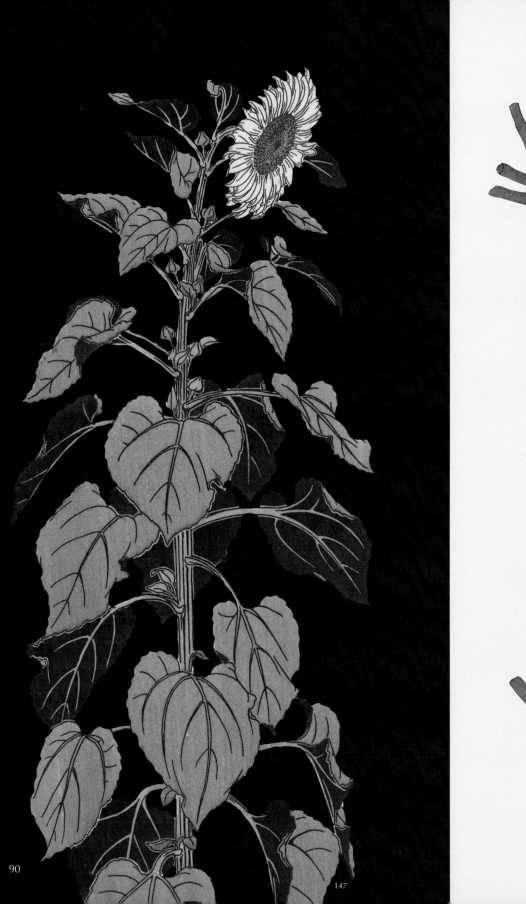

147

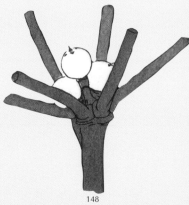

148

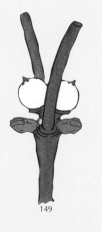

149

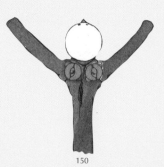

150

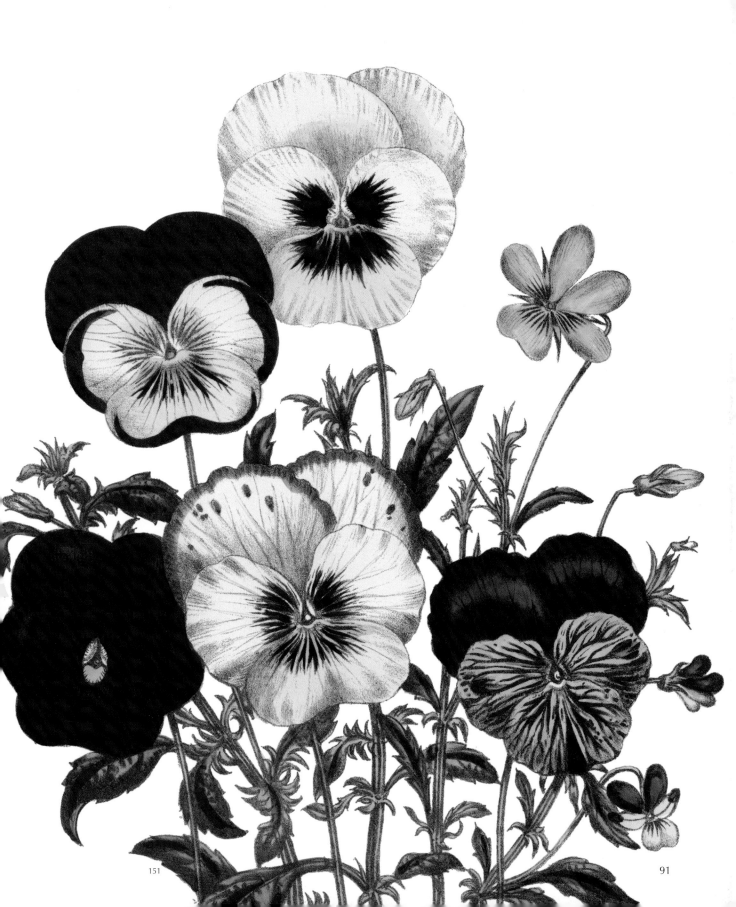

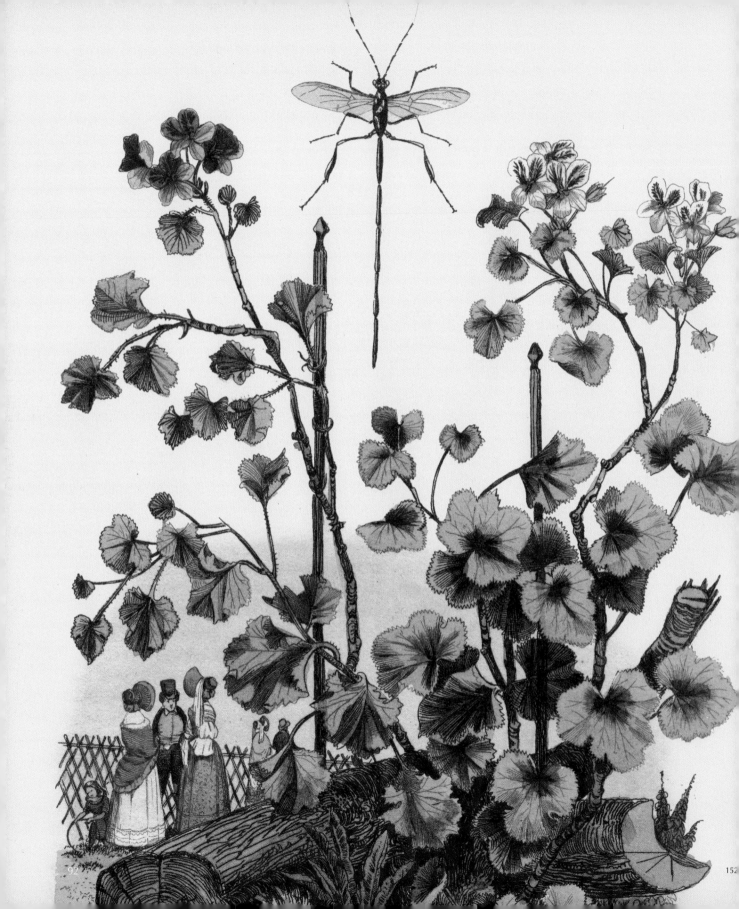

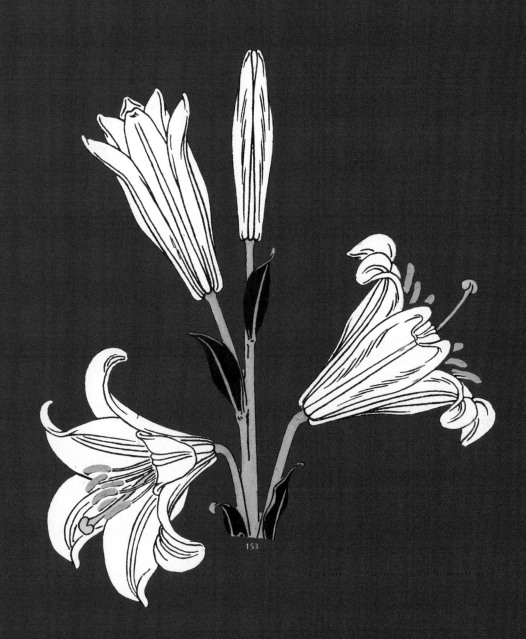

153

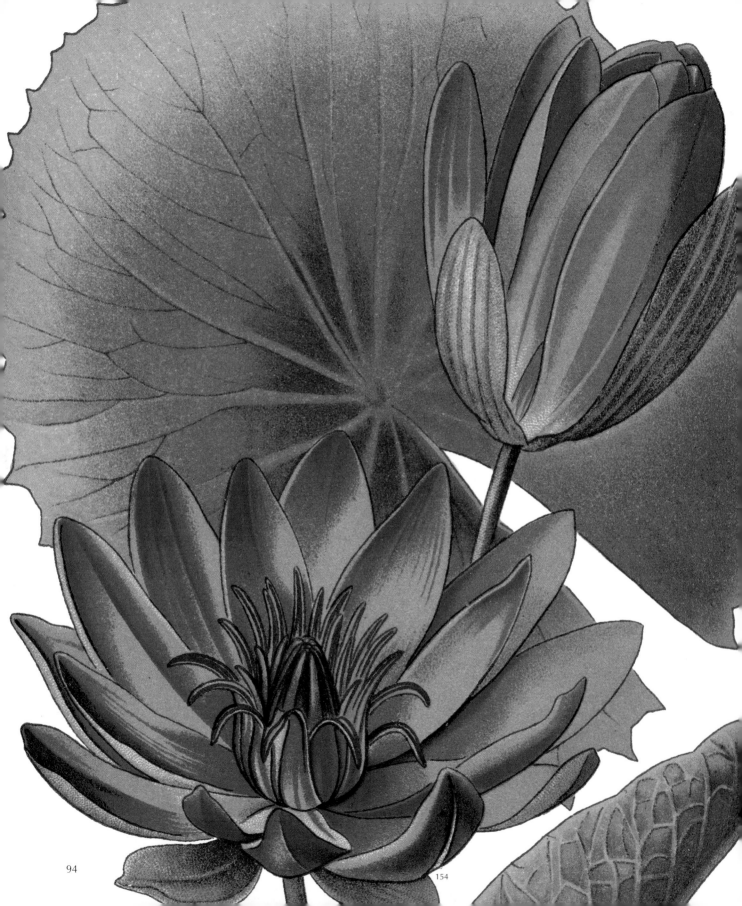

154

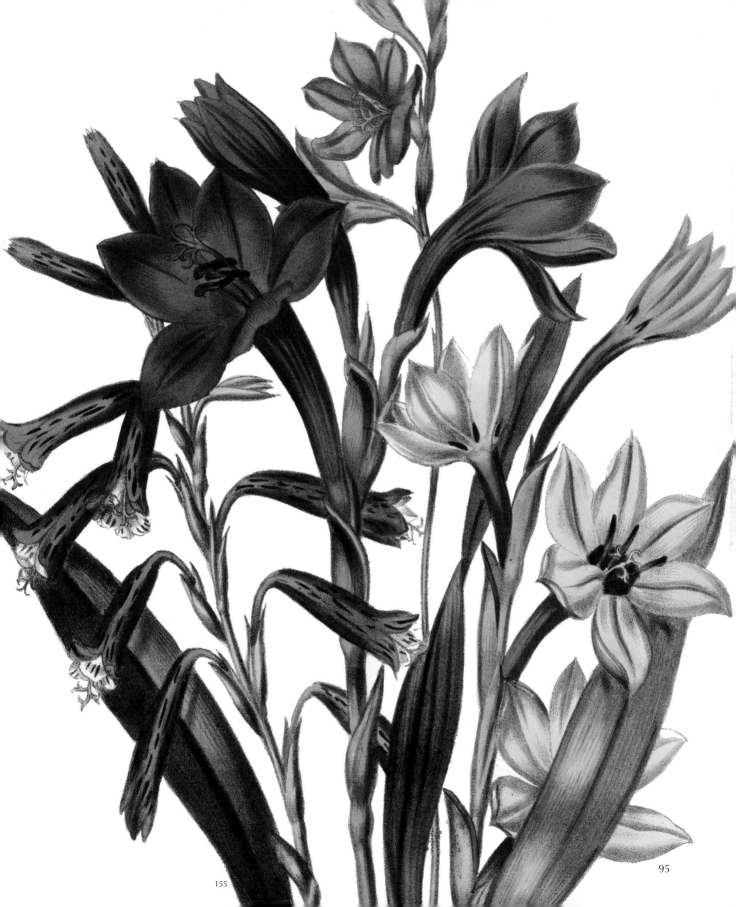

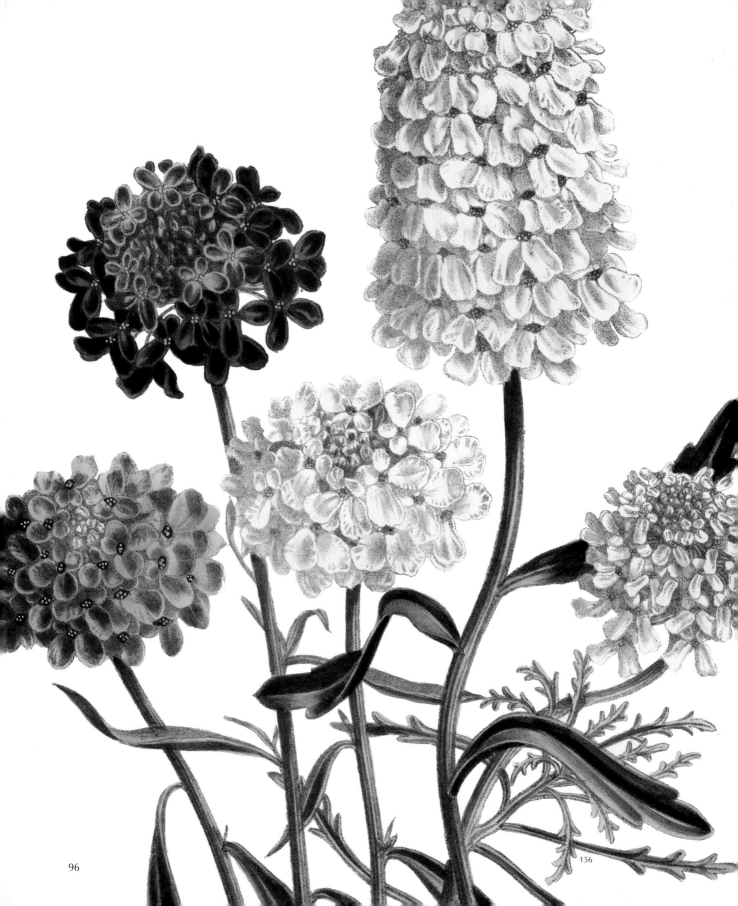

156

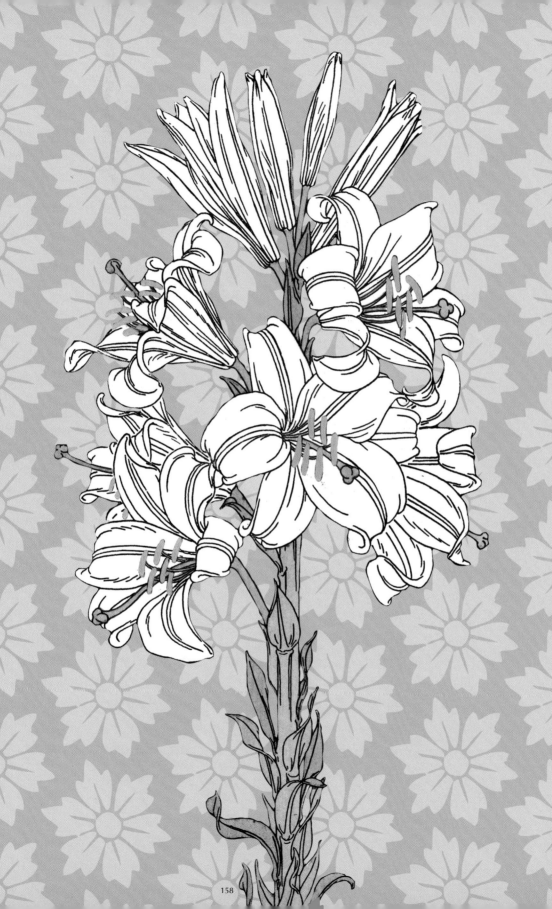

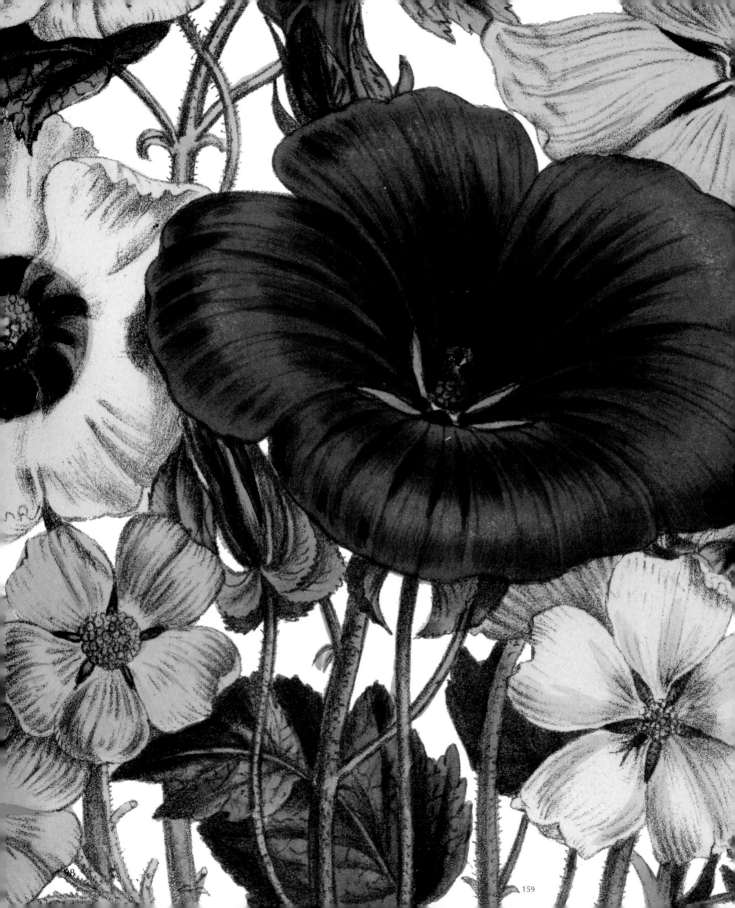

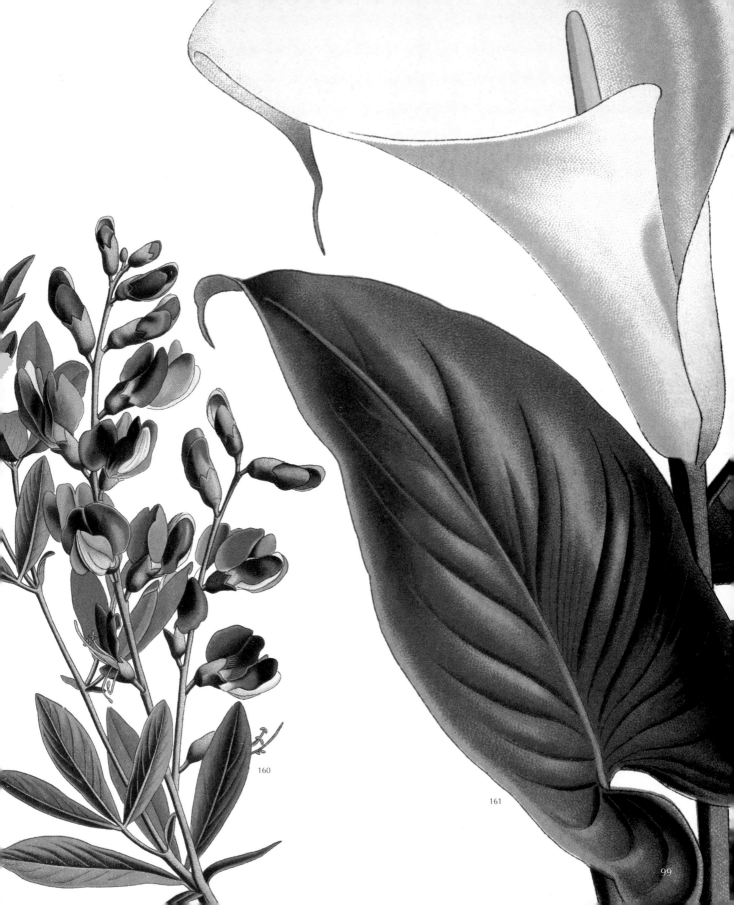

160

161

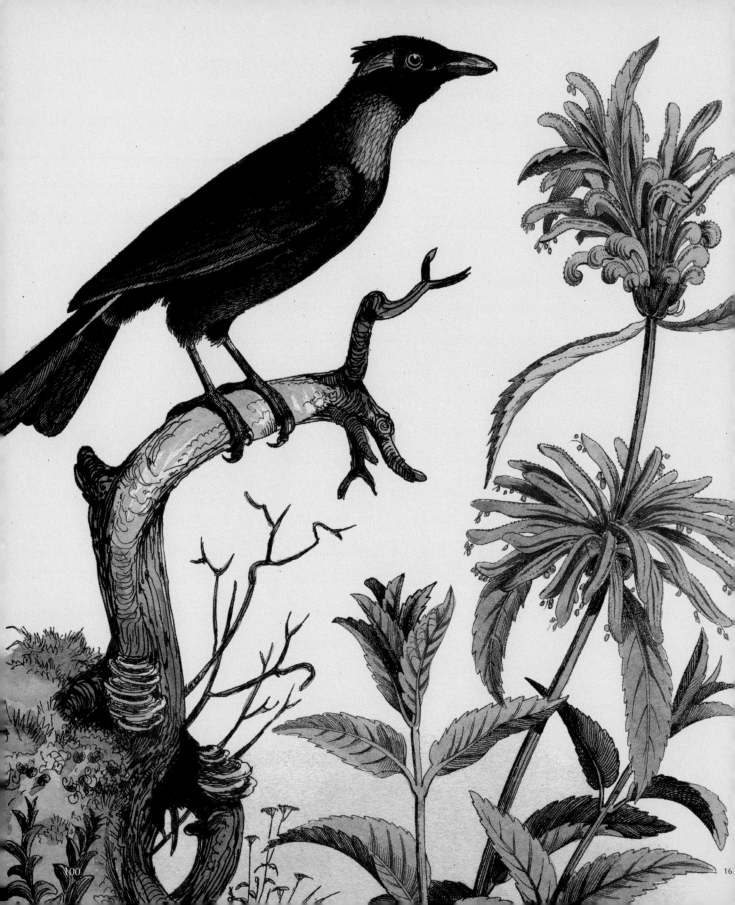

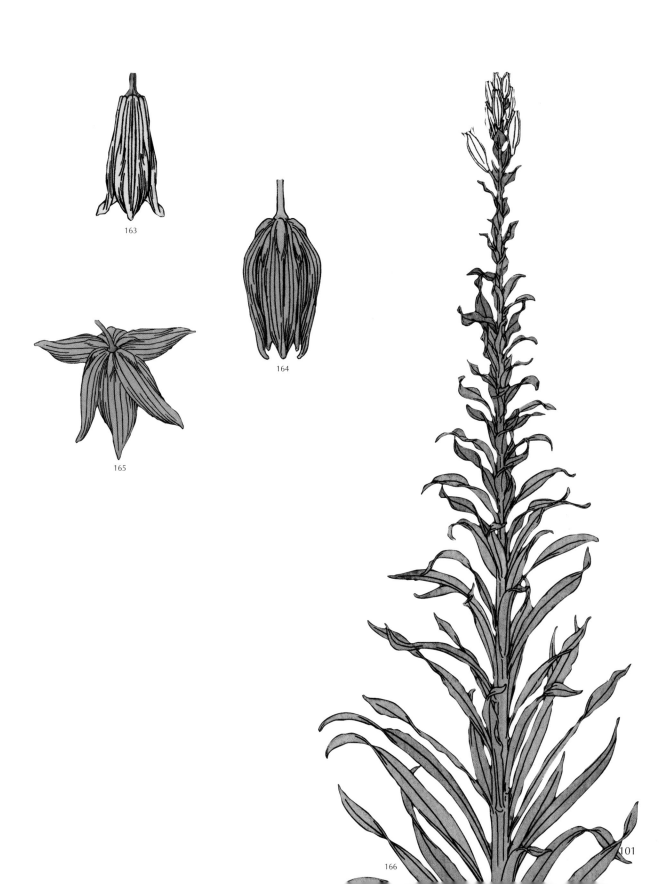

163

164

165

166

101

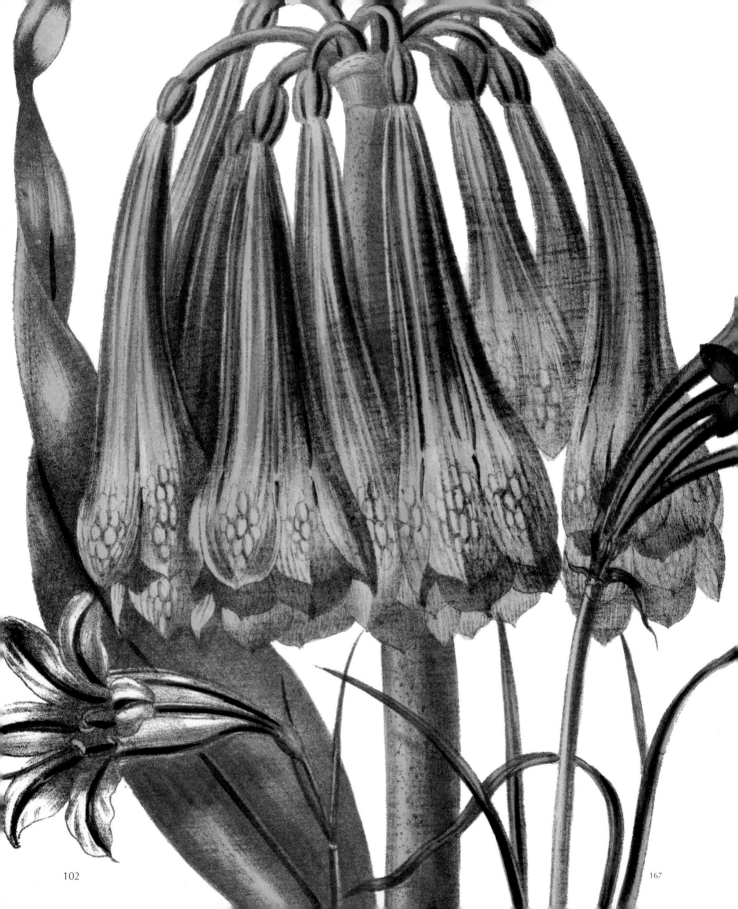

167

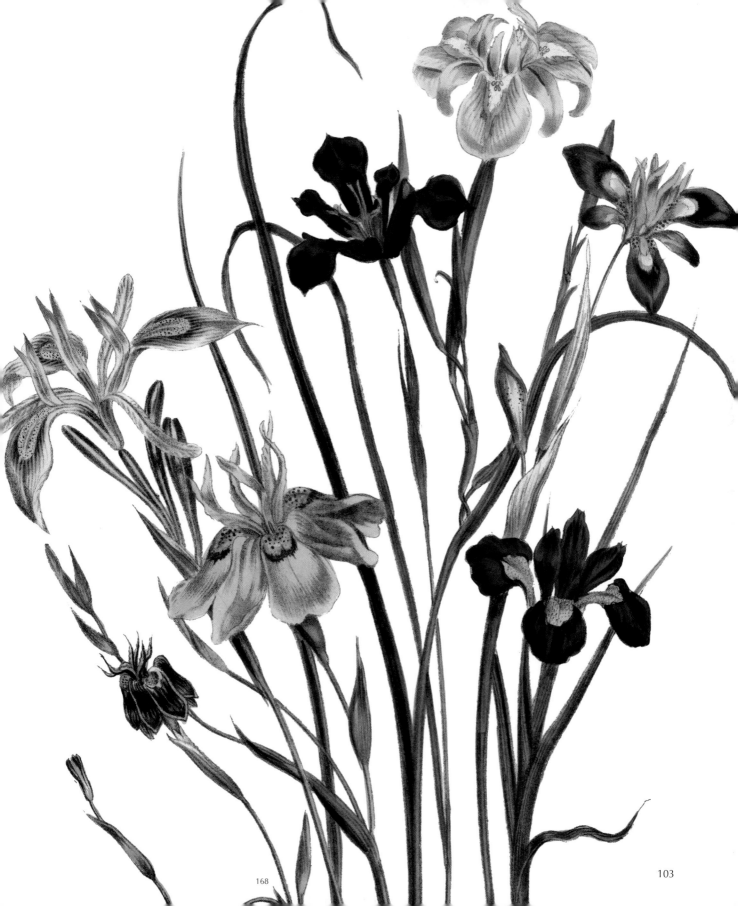

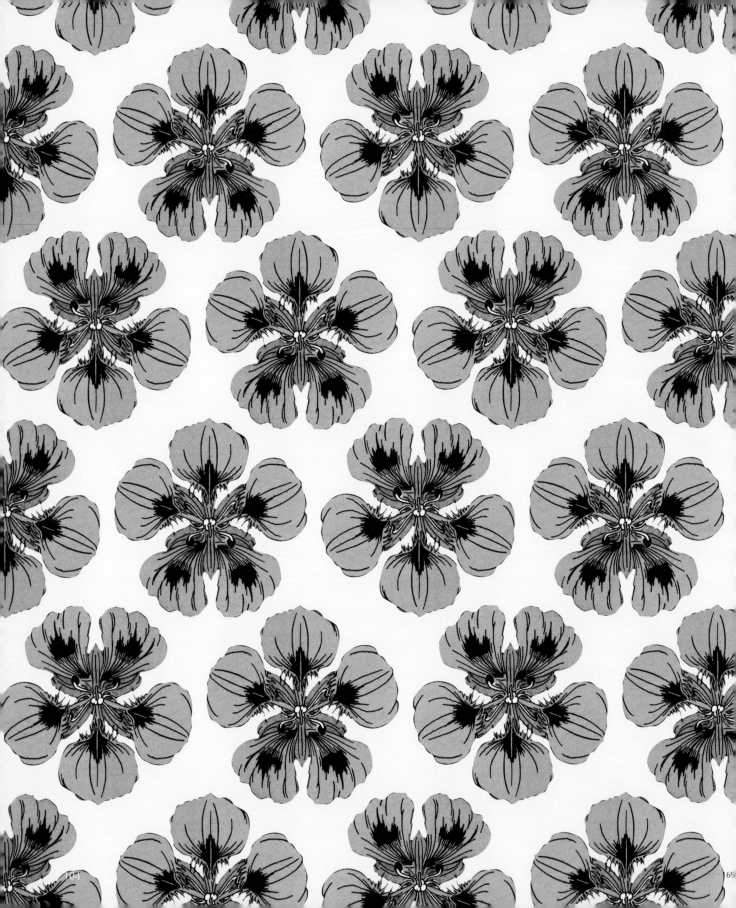

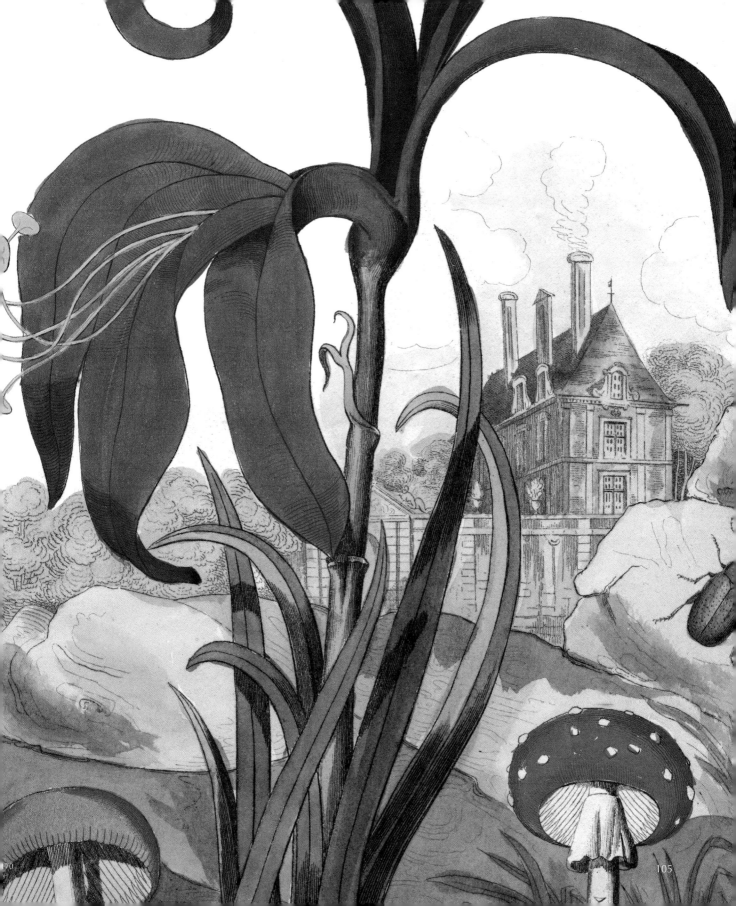

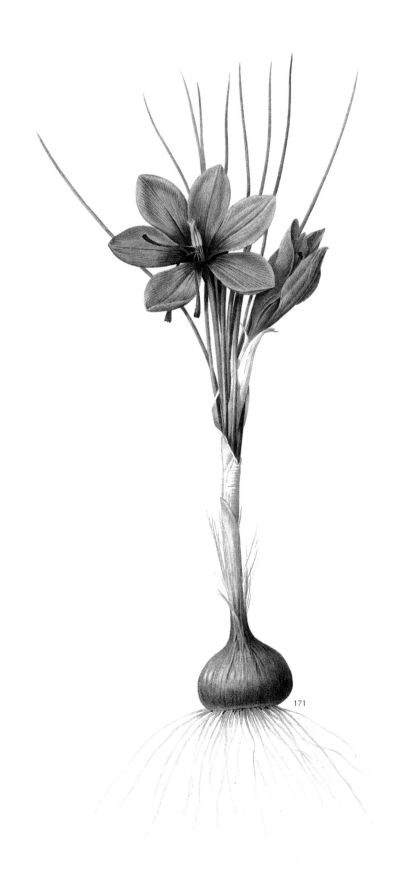

171

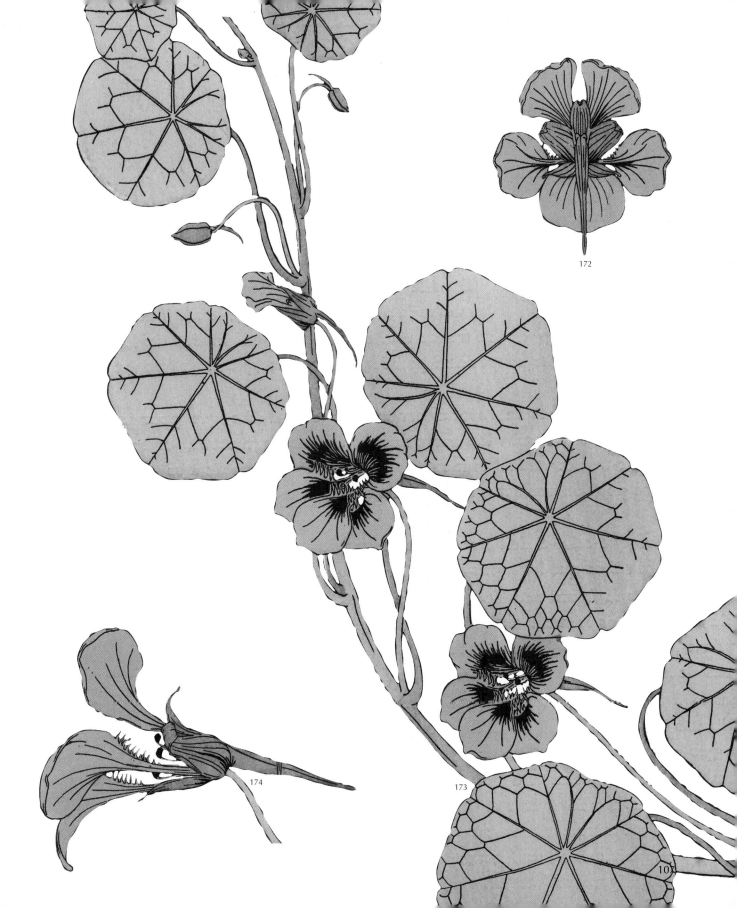

172

174

173

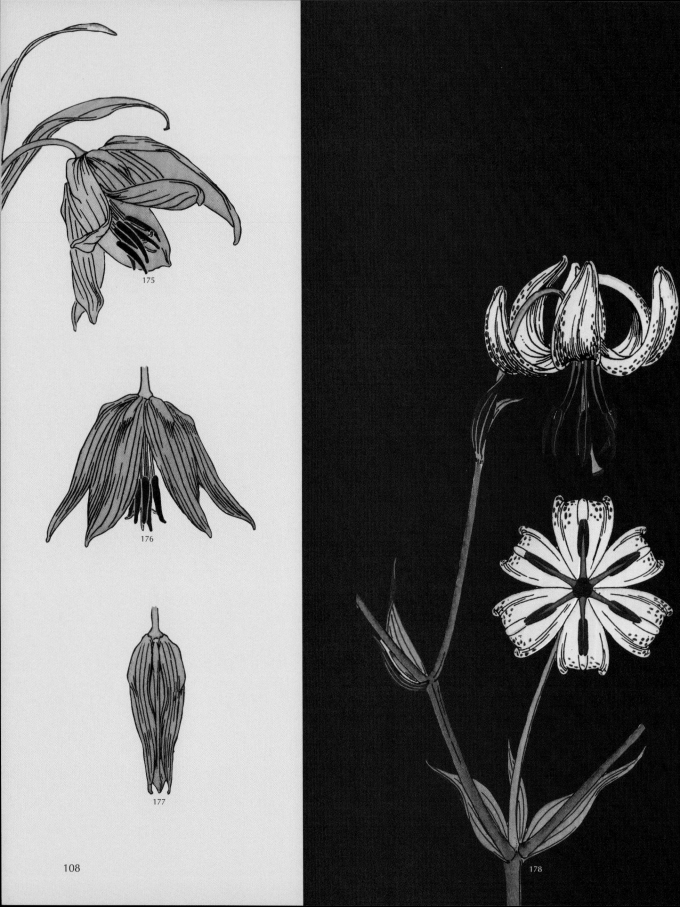

175

176

177

178

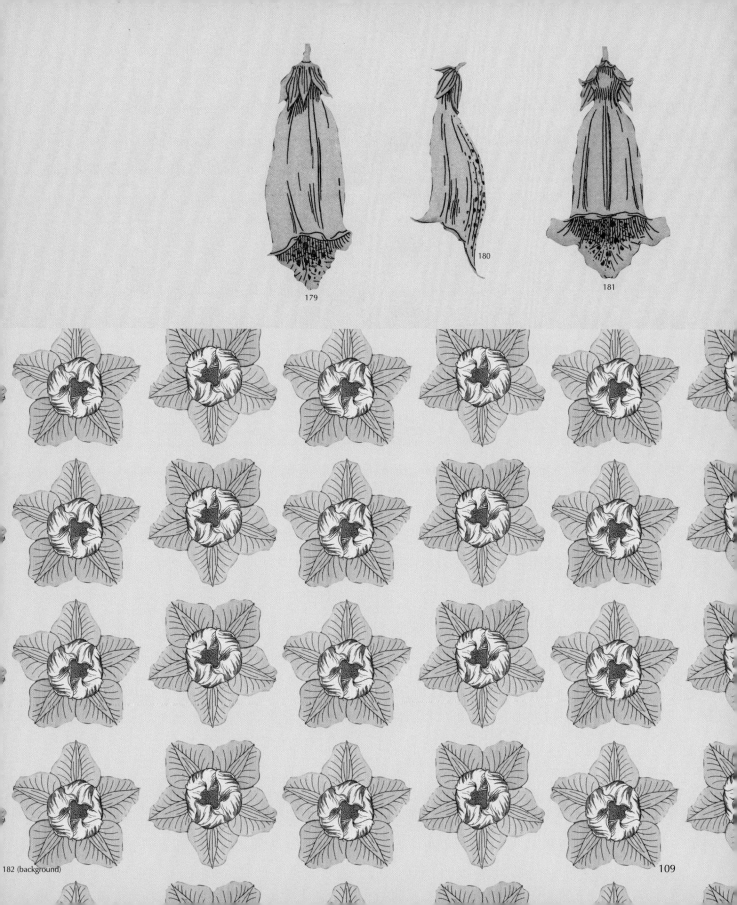

179

180

181

182 (background)

109

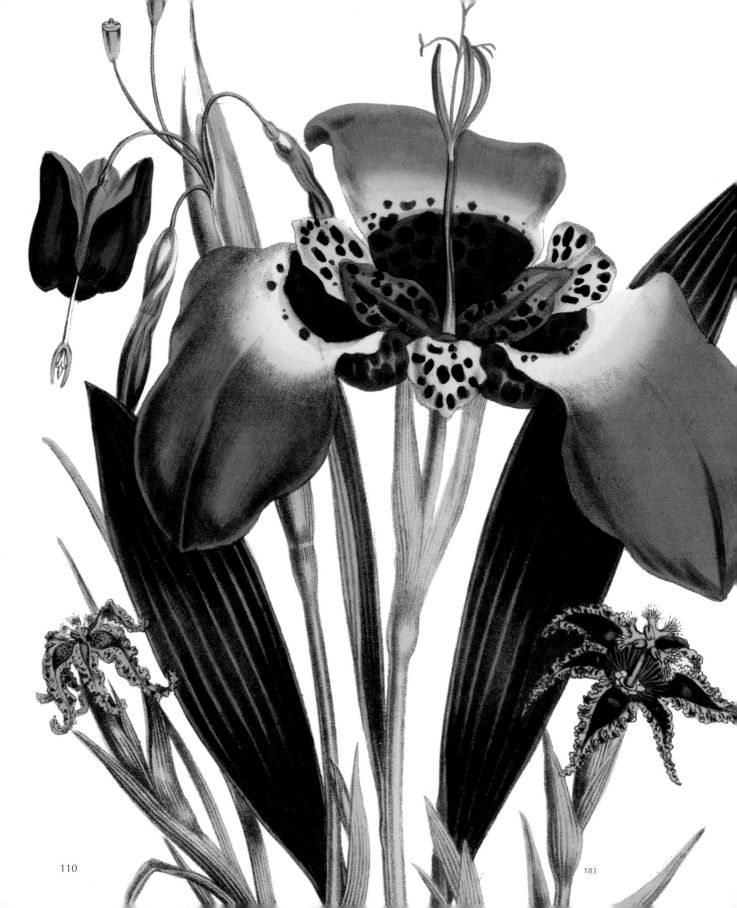

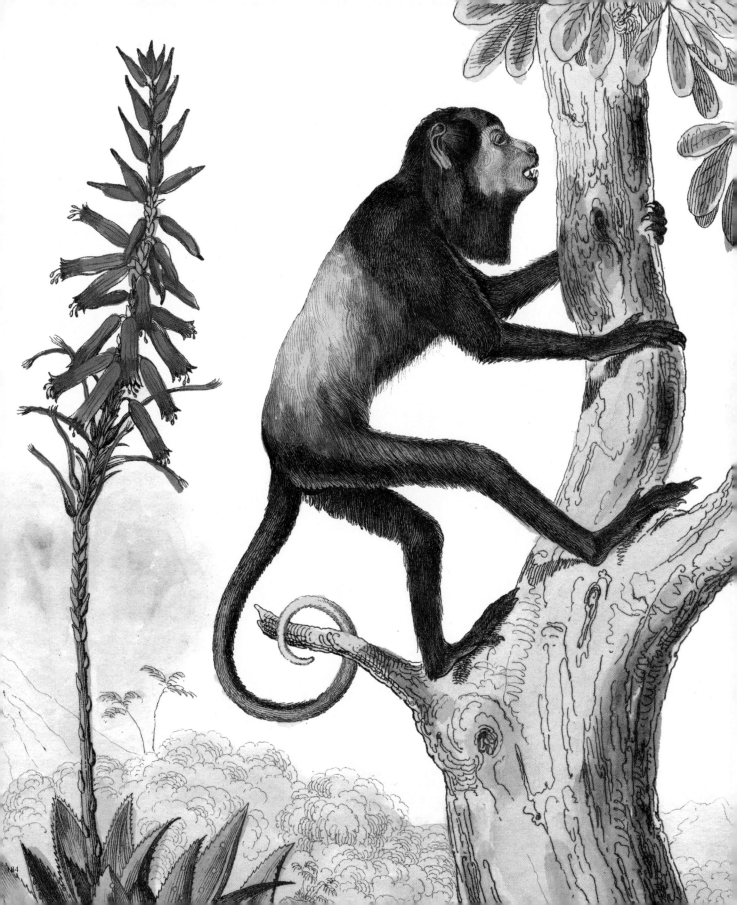

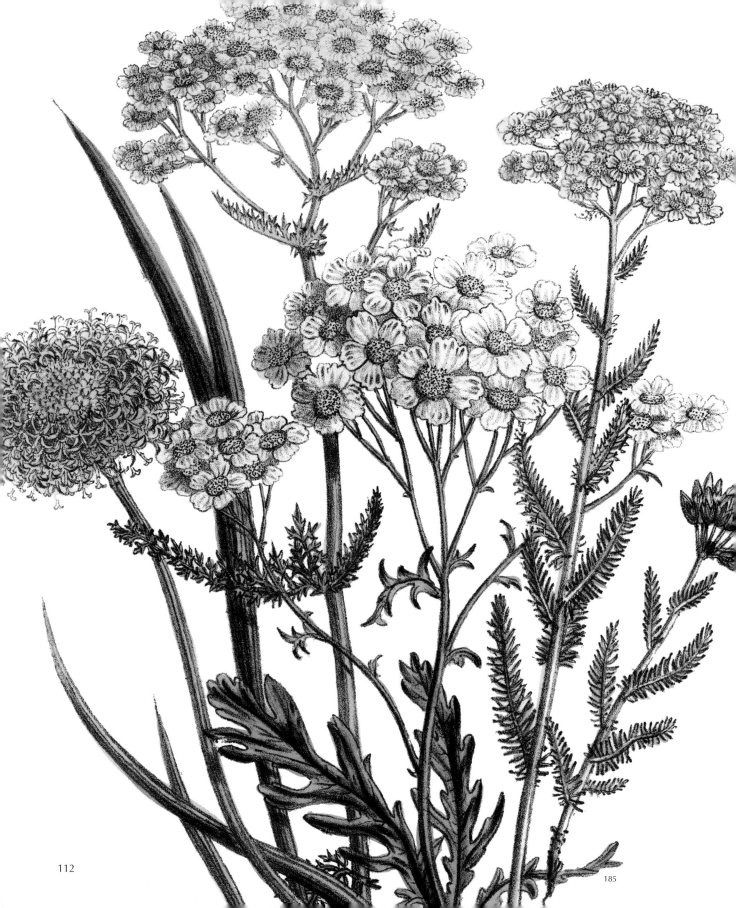

185

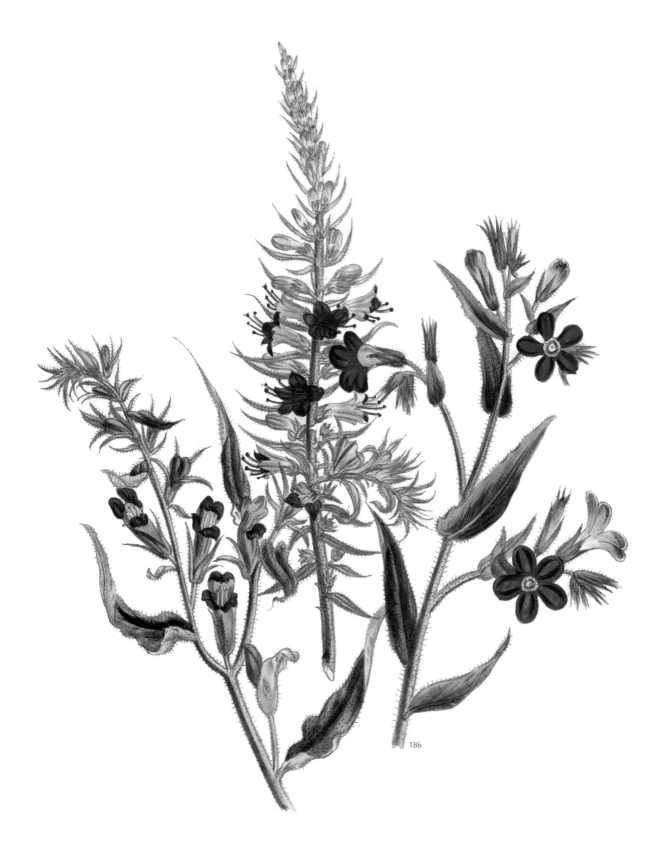

186

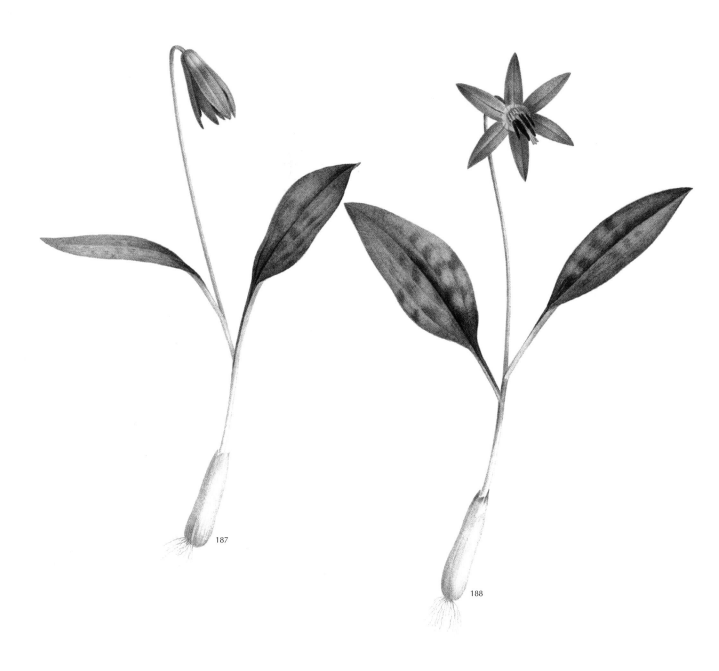

187

188

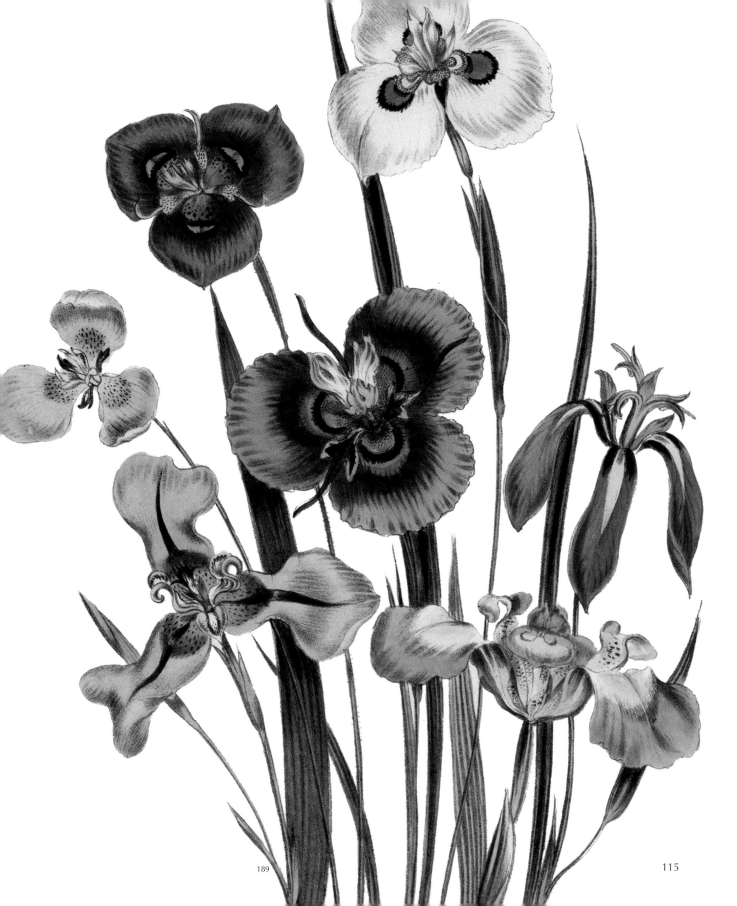

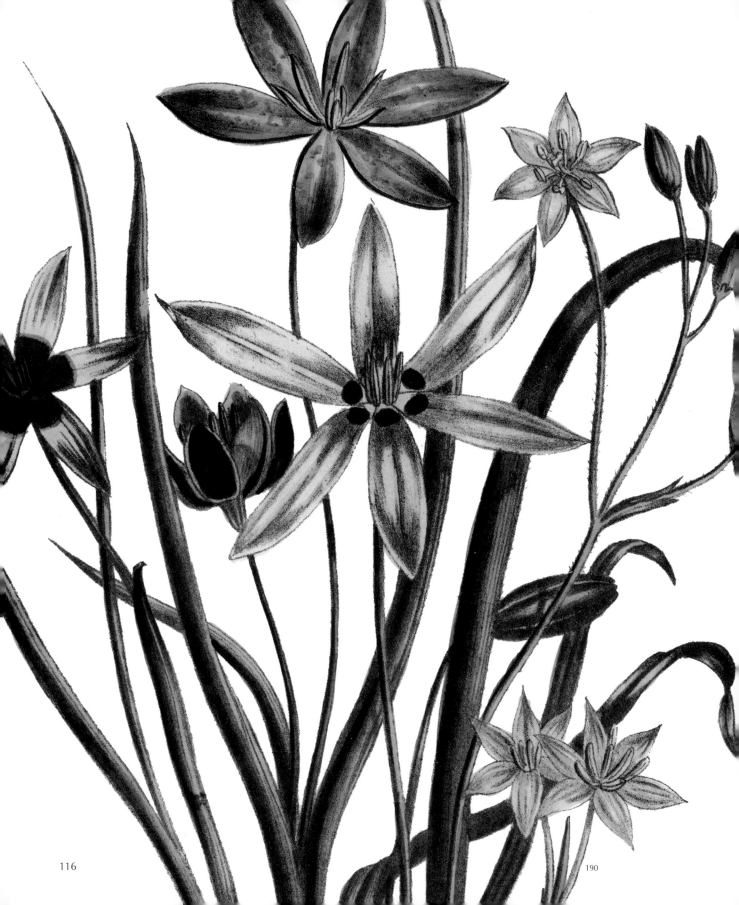

190

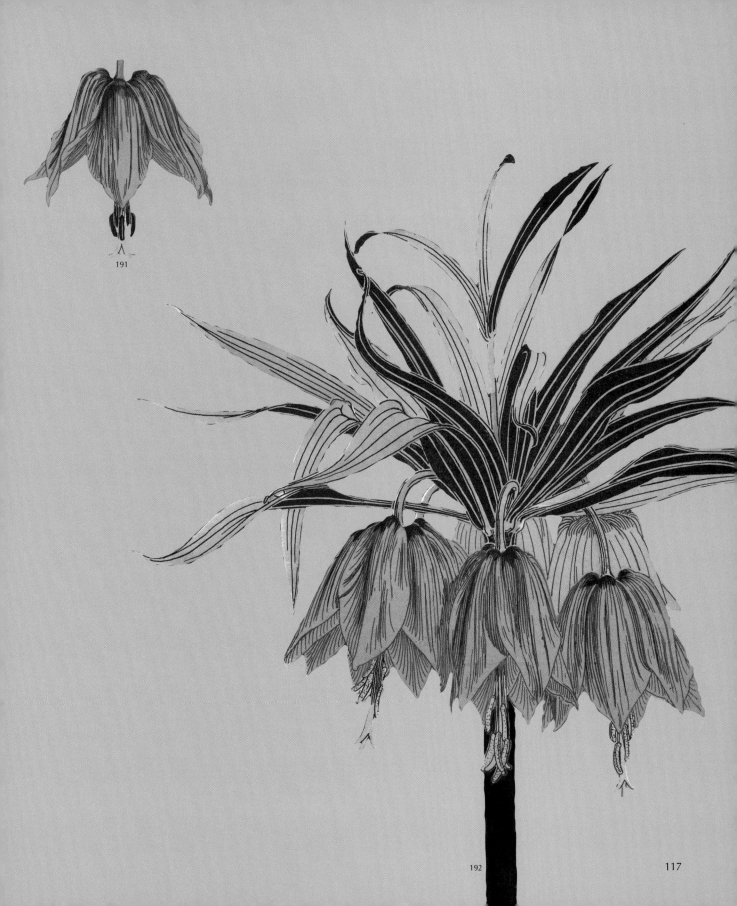

191

192

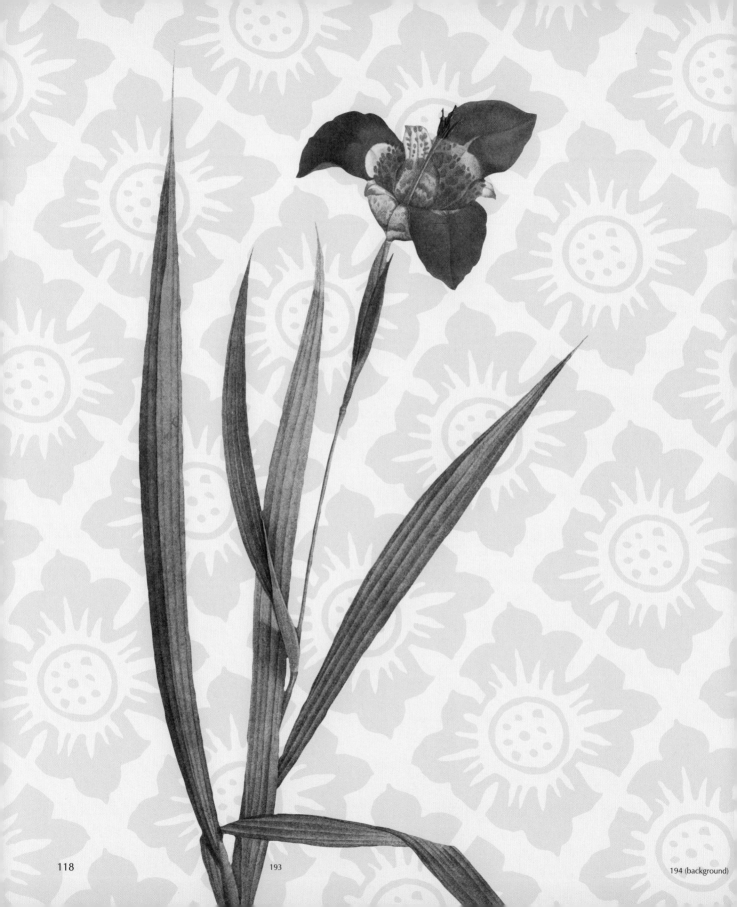

193

194 (background)

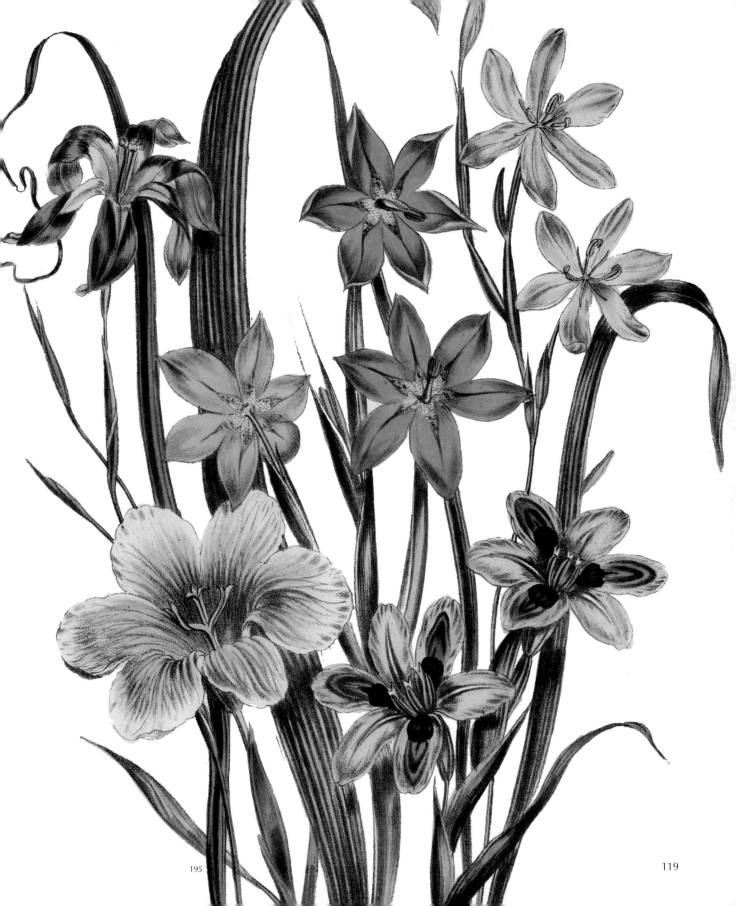

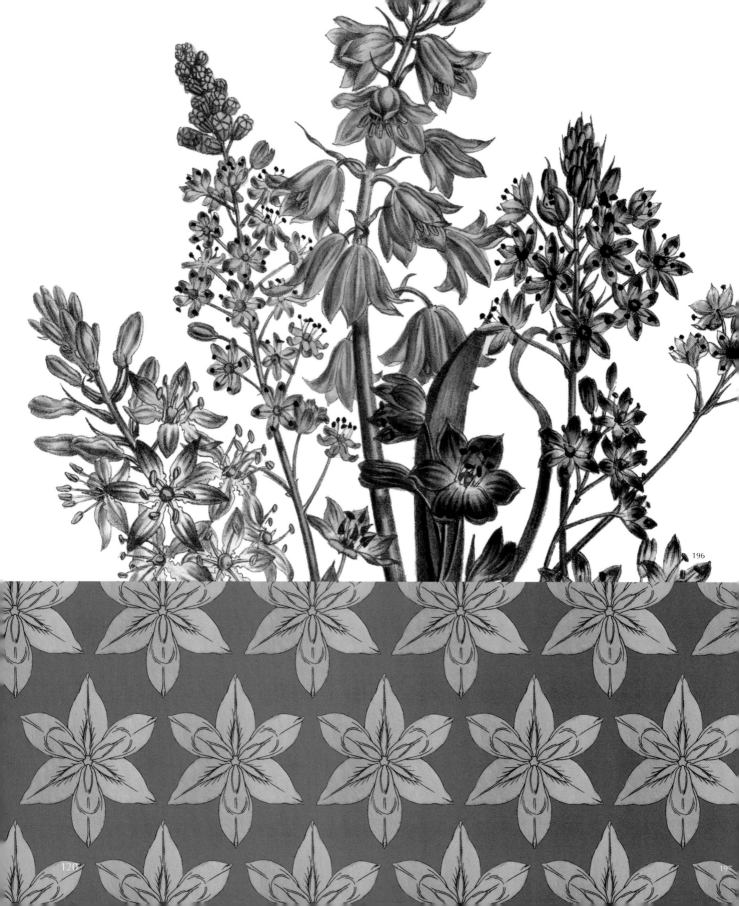

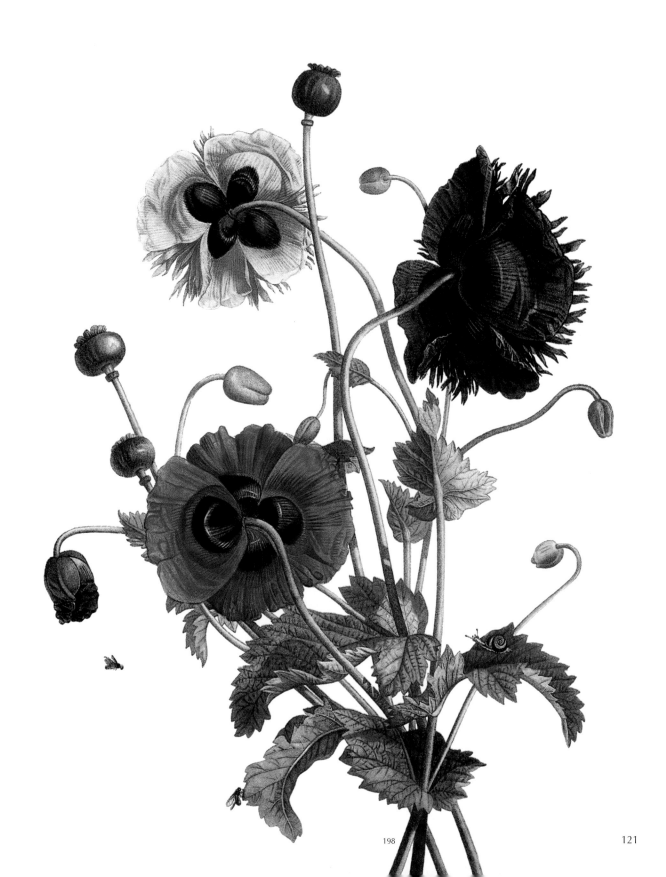

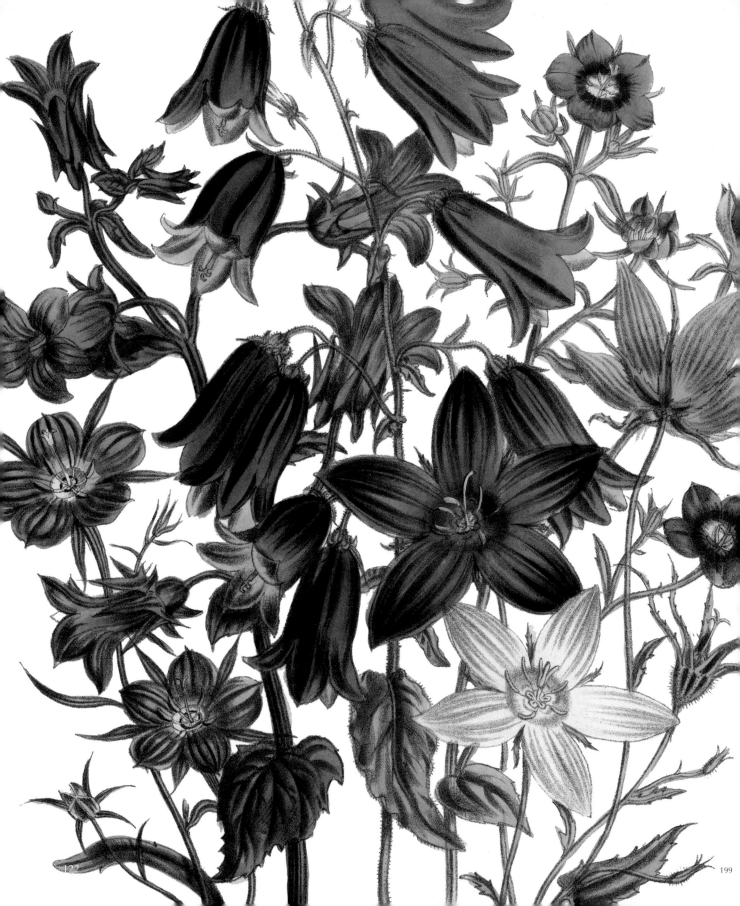

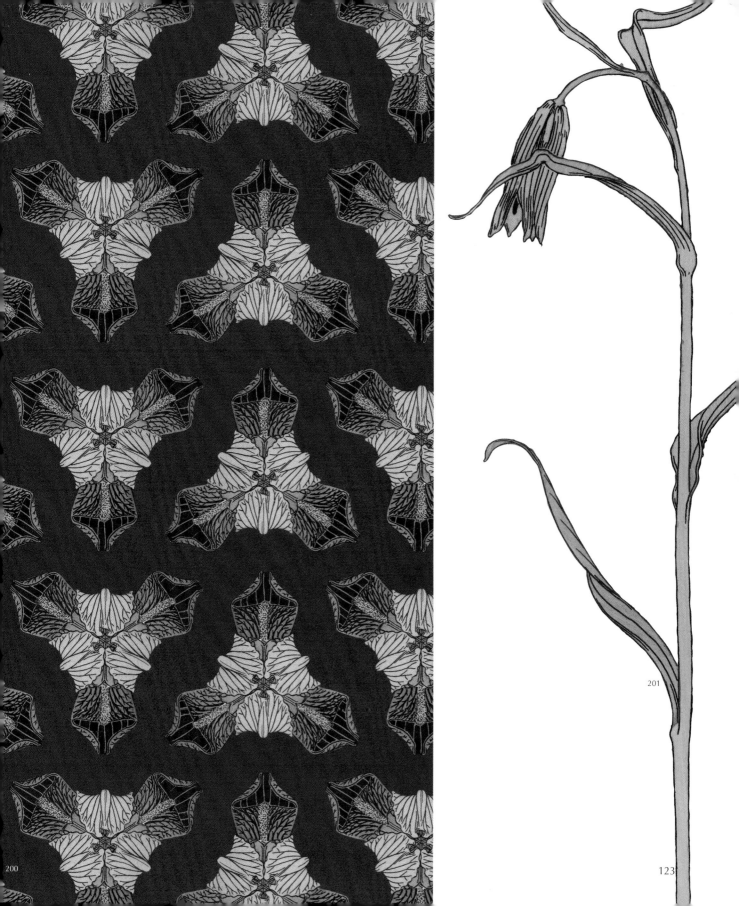

201

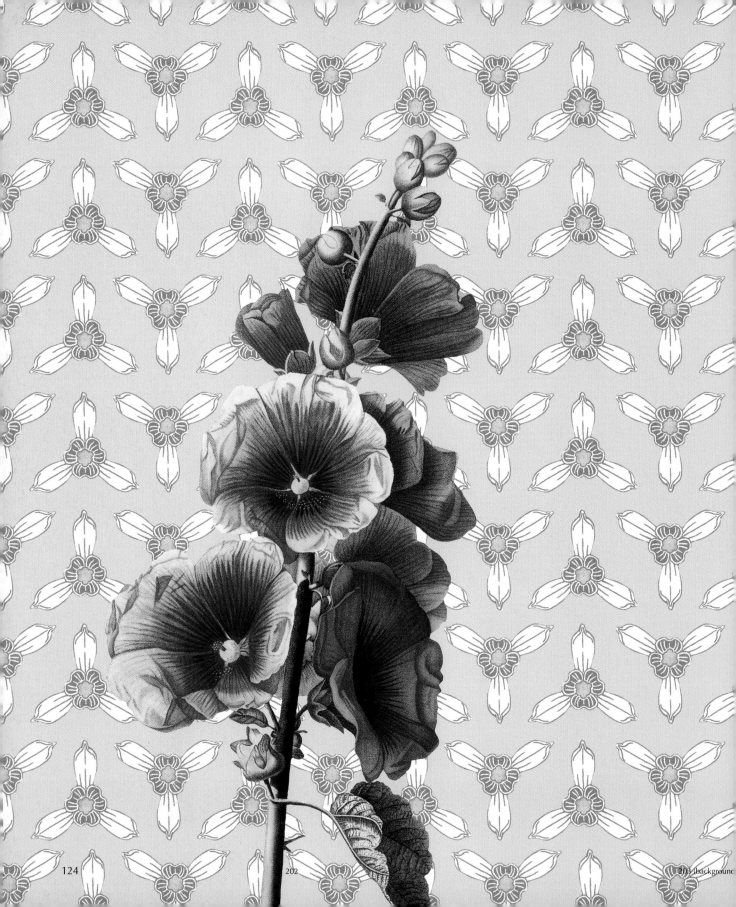

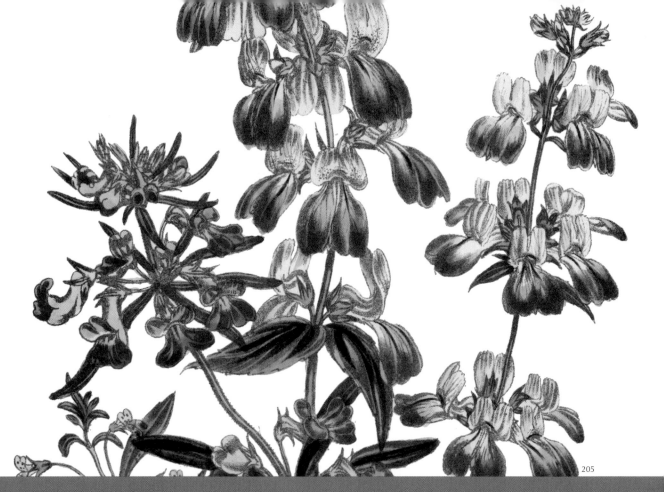

205

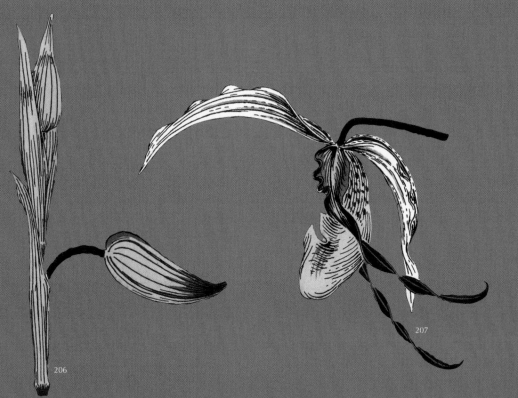

206

207

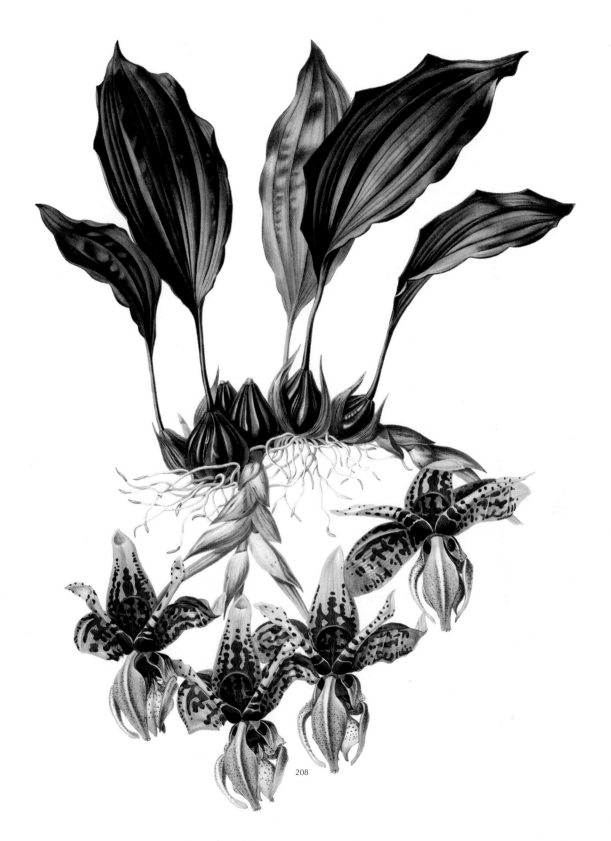

208

List of Vector Images